YAR

MARVELLOUS

The Most Heart-Warming Story Of One Man's triumph
You Will Read This Year

MARVELLOUS

NEIL BALDWIN – MY STORY

With Malcolm Clarke

JOHN BLAKE

Published by John Blake Publishing Ltd,
3 Bramber Court, 2 Bramber Road,
London W14 9PB, England

www.johnblakebooks.com

www.facebook.com/johnblakebooks ⬛
twitter.com/jblakebooks ⬛

This edition published in hardback in 2015

ISBN: 978 1 78418 643 2

British Library Cataloguing-in-Publication Data:

A catalogue record for this book is available from the British Library.

Design by www.envydesign.co.uk

Printed in Great Britain by CPI Group (UK) Ltd

1 3 5 7 9 10 8 6 4 2

Papers used by John Blake Publishing are natural, recyclable products made
from wood grown in sustainable forests. The manufacturing processes
conform to the environmental regulations of the country of origin.

ACKNOWLEDGEMENTS

This book would not have been commissioned if the multi-award-winning BBC TV drama *Marvellous*, based on Neil's life, had not been such an outstanding success. To adapt a line from *Marvellous*: 'Acknowledgements, I wouldn't know where to start.' Or indeed to finish. But I'll try.

We thank the writer and executive director, Peter Bowker, for his brilliantly perceptive and funny script, which truly captured Neil's spirit, so outstandingly portrayed on screen by Toby Jones, without which there would have been no film.

His fellow executive director, Patrick Spence, managing director of Fifty Fathoms, part of the Tiger Aspect group, had the wisdom to see the potential of the film, and sell it to the BBC. He managed the whole process with sensitive professionalism. Patrick was the figurehead and representation of a brilliant directing, production, acting and publicity team, who have gained the professional recognition they so richly deserve, and who had Neil's best interests at the heart of all their work. It seems invidious to selectively name and praise individuals here. Thank you all, guys, for a job superbly well done.

Marvellous itself would not have been conceived and made without the article written about Neil in *The Guardian* in 2010 by our longstanding friend, Francis Beckett. But Francis's contribution certainly did not end there. He conducted some of the interviews for the book, edited the whole text and drew upon his extensive experience as an author and journalist to provide invaluable advice on structure and content, and provided an introduction and afterword. Thank you so much, Francis.

The book tells Neil's extraordinary story, of which I have been privileged to be a part. But I have been only one of many. Over the years, Neil has had hundreds, nay thousands, of friends across the main domains of his life: his family; the church; Keele University; the circus world; Stoke City FC and the wider football world, and the Cambridge University Boat Club. Some of them have contributed directly to the book, and we thank them for their time and co-operation. Many others, only a few of whom are identified in the text, have helped and supported Neil, and he has equally enriched their lives. We extend our thanks to all who have done so, whether or not they are named in the book. You have all been important players in Neil's story.

The editor, Chris Mitchell of John Blake Publishing, and Andy Armitage, the copy editor, have provided invaluably professional input. Sheila Hayward turned my audio tapes into script with remarkable speed and accuracy. John Easom read and provided helpful comments on a draft of the book. Judge Nick Warren allowed me time off from my Information Tribunal duties to work on the book. Thanks to you all, and to anyone else I have inadvertently omitted.

MALCOLM CLARKE

To Dorothy 'Mary' Baldwin
1922–2003
A loving mother whose wisdom, courage and
foresight were truly remarkable.

CONTENTS

FOREWORD
By Francis Beckett

It was one of those occasions the British film industry does well: a glittering preview at the National Film Theatre on the South Bank. Famous actors, footballers and politicians mingled with the crowds, and watched the new film for the very first time before applauding the stars as they walked on stage.

Television presenter Samira Ahmed, who has fronted *PM*, *The World Tonight* and *Sunday Morning Live*, led the way, followed by the stars themselves: Toby Jones, Gemma Jones, Tony Curran, Greg McHugh, with writer Peter Bowker and director Julian Farino. They started to talk, but there was still a sense of expectation. Something was missing.

Then a short, stout, late-middle-aged man walked on stage, using a walking stick because of a recent hip operation. His round face was covered by the widest and happiest smile we had seen for a while, and he spoke in a gravelly and curiously flat voice with a strong Potteries accent.

He was wearing a dinner jacket, in stark contrast to the elaborately casual clothes of the metropolitan elite around him, but clearly didn't feel at all overdressed. In fact, everyone else suddenly felt a bit *underdressed*, and Samira Ahmed said, 'You're the only person here who's dressed properly.'

His name was Neil Baldwin, and the film was a fictionalised version of his life.

It's a name everyone now feels they know, but can't quite pin down. Is he Neil Baldwin the cabinet minister, or Neil Baldwin the famous writer, or the actor or the talk-show host or the footballer, or the latest winner of *Celebrity Big Brother?*

It has been like that for more than half a century. When eighteen-year-old Malcolm Clarke arrived for his first day at Keele University in 1964, a short, stout young man wearing a clerical collar came up to him and said, 'Welcome to Keele. I'm Neil Baldwin.' Fifty years later, Malcolm wrote, 'I appreciated his warm welcome, but just who was he? As always with Neil, his exact status seemed uncertain.'

It was still like that in 2010, when I profiled him for *The Guardian*. The profile inspired the film *Marvellous*, which was broadcast in 2014.

So who is Neil Baldwin, and why does he matter? To understand that, you have to understand his singular life, and in this book Neil and Malcolm, with a little help from me, guide you through it. Maybe, when you come to the end, you will feel you understand; and maybe not. But you will feel more optimistic, because that's what exposure to Neil does.

CHAPTER ONE

NEIL'S FIRST CELEBRITY: THE ENGLAND FOOTBALLER WHO SIGNED HIS BIRTH CERTIFICATE

NEIL

There's two things I want to tell you at the start. First, I like to remember the happy things. I put nasty things behind me. And, second, you can get things by asking for them. I always do.

I was born on 15 March 1946. Mum and Dad were both big Stoke City – or Potters – supporters, so they named me after Neil Franklin, who was the Stoke City centre-half in 1946. He was quite a player, Neil Franklin. He played for England twenty-seven times in a row and, if he hadn't been silly enough to go to Colombia, he would have been the first player to get a hundred England caps. The day after I was born, Franklin turned out for Stoke City in an away game at Grimsby Town, which we won 2–0. I've been a winner ever since.

My mum and dad even got him to write a message on the back of my birth certificate, too. It says, 'With very best wishes from Neil Franklin, Stoke City FC and England.' I'm very proud of that. Of course, I've got to know a lot more famous people since then.

MALCOLM

Neil was the only child of Mary and Harry Baldwin who were married in October 1944, when Harry, an engineering fitter, was thirty-one, and Mary was a few days short of her twenty-second birthday. They settled in a prefabricated bungalow in Chesterton, a working-class suburb of Newcastle-under-Lyme, the so-called 'Loyal and Ancient Borough' next to the city of Stoke-on-Trent.

Mary didn't have an easy pregnancy. One family story has it that, because of a fear that she might miscarry, she was given an injection she shouldn't have had, which caused the 'learning difficulties' or 'special needs' that Neil was once labelled as having.

We'll never know for certain. But, if a clinical mistake *was* responsible for Neil's total lack of the embarrassment, self-consciousness and fear of artificial social niceties that often hold most of us back from doing the things we want to do, then it's not such a bad thing, is it?

NEIL

I don't know anything about an injection, but I'm not worried about that. All I know is that I came out OK and I've had a great life and I've always been very happy. I've become a film star. Not many people have a film made about their life, do they? And I've got an honorary degree, which not many people have.

MALCOLM

Harry Baldwin, who was born in Wolstanton, Newcastle-under-Lyme, came from a North Staffordshire working-class family. His mother died when he was five. His father, Neil's grandfather, Thomas Baldwin, was a miner who died when Neil was eleven. He lived just down the road from Neil in Chesterton, as did Neil's great-uncle, Dan Johnson, his wife, Lilian, and his son, also called Dan.

Uncle Dan recalls the family and Neil's childhood:

> Harry was a fine chap but was very quiet. He was a singer in the local church choir, as was Neil. Neil's always been a good singer.
>
> Some ignorant people in the area didn't have much to do with Neil because they said he was slow. He was always polite and very respectful, which he got from Mary. If Neil ever crossed the line, Mary would firmly say, 'Neil – that will do. No more.'
>
> He didn't ask for anything, but somehow before he left the room he would always get what he wanted, and that has carried on through his life – look at the autographs he's got and the famous people he's met.

NEIL

When I was about six, the teachers sent me to a speech therapist because my voice wasn't working properly. I had to go to the hospital every week to learn how to speak. There was someone asking me questions and I'd have to answer. They wanted to get me to speak right.

I went for about two years and then it was all right and I didn't have to go any more. There was no problem with reading. I was a great reader.

I went to the local primary school in Chesterton. It was in a very old building. I quite liked it. There was a teacher called Mr Dowler who was always very nice to me. Some of them *weren't* nice to me, and I got into trouble sometimes.

They decided not to bother to sit me for the eleven-plus, and I went to Broad Meadow, the local secondary modern school. Uncle Dan still calls it the 'college of knowledge'. Yes, of course there was a bit of bullying there, but I was all right, I stood up for myself.

MALCOLM

Neil was a friend of the late Gilbert Bartels, who was also regarded as having special needs. Gilbert's brother Paul recalls:

Gilbert and Neil were like each other in many ways. Both of them always saw the best in people, even if they weren't treated right. Because they were seen as being limited, they were picked on by the school bullies and had the mickey taken out of them by the local kids. It was quite a tough area to grow up in, but it didn't seem to faze Neil.

I liked Neil because he always did what he wanted to do once he set his mind on something. Sometimes his mum had difficulty in stopping him if there was something he really wanted to do.

He was very involved with the local church even as a young boy. He used to wear a large wooden cross about five inches by three inches round his neck, which was a very unusual thing to do.

NEIL

You should never be afraid to proclaim your faith. Christ died on the cross for us.

MALCOLM

David Kelsall was a student teacher at Broadmeadow in 1959–60. He recalls:

The school had four streams, A, B, C and D. Neil was in D stream, and academically probably at the bottom of that. Their class teacher was Ron Cauldwell, who taught every subject. Ron was an inspirational teacher who had a really good personality for teaching, and a real commitment to help the less academically able kids. The school could be quite brutal but Ron didn't use the cane like other teachers. Neil couldn't have been in better hands.

Before I took the class, I remember Ron telling me, 'Don't worry about Neil. He'll do his best and do what he can. He won't cause you any problems.' I just remember Neil as a really nice pleasant lad who was always smiling. He was always smart with a tie on and he often wore a green jacket.

NEIL

I remember David. He was very nice. Ron Cauldwell was a great teacher who looked after me. He taught our class for two or three years. Mr Toms was the head teacher and he was a nice man.

MALCOLM

David Leech, another local contemporary, who eventually went on to be the leader of the local council, also remembers the strength of Neil's religious commitment. 'Neil always walked round the village with a large Bible under his arm,' he told me. Bert Proctor, three years Neil's senior, also remembers Neil's Bible and comments:

> He would give you the impression that he had an official role with the church, but that was really due to innocent simplicity, not an attempt to deceive you. The clergy had no choice but to get to know Neil, because, once Neil had decided that it was worth getting in with somebody, he was always confident enough to do so. That came from his mum. It's interesting that I remember her well but not his dad.
>
> Neil knew everybody in Chesterton and everybody knew him. He was uncomplicated, with no hidden agendas and didn't take offence. He became interested in and visited the churches and the university, whereas Gilbert did the same in the hospital. Today's society with its concerns about security and other things wouldn't be so

accommodating. I worked in a butcher's shop after I left school and Neil was also very interested in that.

Uncle Dan also recalls Neil's early self-confidence:

He once asked me to phone Sandhurst to get him some application forms to join the military academy, which of course I did and he got the forms, but he became a clown instead.

His son, Young Dan, thirteen years Neil's junior, recalls being taken to Stoke City as a young child by Neil:

We hung around for ages after the game getting players' autographs. Neil coached me how to ask for autographs. He had no fear. Once, he just walked into the players' bar. I was embarrassed and just wanted to get out but Neil wasn't bothered at all.

Uncle Dan recalls family trips to West Midlands Safari Park at Bewdley in Mary's car, when Neil was in his twenties and Young Dan was a teenager, but his boldness caused them worry: 'Neil was always winding down the window in the lions' enclosure, which frightened us all. He was obsessed with animals.'

Young Dan recalls that Mary's driving added to the concern:

We were always scared Mary would stall the car whilst we were in a dangerous-animal enclosure and Neil would open the door. She had trouble finding the gears in her Renault 5. She wasn't a very good driver. We used to go to the country, to Dovedale. I remember Neil just climbing right up the rocks with ordinary shoes on. He was fearless and had an amazing amount of energy.

NEIL

We Baldwins were a very close family. I used to see Uncle Dan and his family a lot because they lived just round the corner but for a long time I used to call him 'Mr Johnson' because no one realised until much later that my grandmother, who had died, was the sister of Uncle Dan's father. Mum and Dad always taught me to be very polite to the neighbours. As well as Uncle Dan's family, my granddad lived just down the road from us in Chesterton as well as my uncle Eddie, who was also very good to me. Everyone lived nearby and I had a very happy childhood. I have always loved the trips to the safari park and the country. They were marvellous.

I had some good friends. I wasn't bullied at school and I never used to worry about what some of the other kids in Chesterton said to me. I took no notice. That happens to everyone. I was very happy and I still am and have always been proud to be a Christian.

MALCOLM

Mary had been born in October 1922 in Birkenhead. Her mother, Sarah, died in 1929, aged thirty-four, after giving birth to five children in five years, one of whom died in childbirth. Mary, the second of four surviving children, was only seven. So both Neil's parents had suffered the loss of their mothers at a very early age.

NEIL

Because he was in the navy my granddad couldn't cope with looking after my mum and her two sisters and one brother and the family was split up.

MALCOLM

Mary's sister Iris and Iris's twin brother Dennis were sent to an orphanage, where they suffered some cruel treatment. Dennis eventually became an alcoholic and moved away. When he did return, on one occasion around 1970, Neil's granddad disowned him and wouldn't even tell him where his sisters were living. Iris named her daughter, Denise, Neil's cousin, after Dennis, and, despite Iris's lifelong attempts to find her twin brother, his sisters never saw him again. In 2012, after Iris and Mary had both died, a company of heir hunters who were trying to find the beneficiaries of Dennis's estate tracked down Denise, who learned that Dennis had died in a hostel in Darlington in 2006.

Mary had a much better deal than the twins: she was sent to live with well-off relatives, first in a posh part of Birmingham and then at Prees in Shropshire, and had private schooling. Perhaps this partly explains the self-confidence she had in dealing with people from a variety of backgrounds, and her resilience, both of which qualities she certainly passed on to Neil.

Her father eventually remarried, and I think she returned to live with him when she was aged about sixteen, and got a job as a silver-service waitress. Within about six years she was married. During the war she worked as an inspector in a munitions factory – of which there were several in North Staffordshire – which she enjoyed, and it seems most likely that she met Harry there. She gave the job up when she got married to become a traditional housewife at home.

NEIL

She was a marvellous mum who always looked after me well. It's very sad that she lost contact with her brother and never saw him again and I had an uncle who I never met.

When I was thirteen, in 1959, I was taken ill with pneumonia, and I was off school for several weeks. It was quite hard coming back: I'd missed a lot of lessons and it wasn't easy to catch up. But I was OK. They made me a prefect – I had to look after the little kids and try to be friendly to them. I liked doing that. I've always liked doing that.

Some of those kids still see me in town, in Newcastle-under-Lyme. They say, 'Hey, Neil, I was at school with you.' I heard the other day in town that one of the teachers there, Ron Stanton, was asking after me, and he's eighty-one now. He was head of RE and he was always very nice to me. My parents were strong Christians, as well as Stoke City supporters, and so am I.

MALCOLM

Neil's cousin Denise says:

When our Neil was young, my mother used to say to Mary, 'Something's not right: he's not developing, not sitting up or walking when he should.' But Mary would not accept that anything was wrong. Harry realised but he kept very quiet. It was only much later that Mary accepted that things were not quite normal, but she never let it affect anything and always believed our Neil could do whatever he wanted. And he has! The only label I have ever given our Neil is 'cousin', and the same goes for all the family. I just think of my mum, Mary, myself, and Neil as being very alike – never seeing the bad in people.

When I was a child we had so many lovely times with our Neil, who was so much fun for my sister Brenda and myself. He was in his teens but we were younger. When we went to Chesterton, we spent hours in the park opposite where they lived in Ripon Avenue, or, when they came here, we went to the Stanley Street park. Some of the local kids in Chesterton used to call him unpleasant names such as 'spastic', but it just never bothered him. Life never seems to bother him.

Denise's sister Brenda recalls:

When we were children I spent a lot of time playing with Neil when we visited Auntie Mary and Uncle Harry. Neil was always so comical. He has no inhibitions. If he wants something he just asks for it. Auntie Mary was such a lovely lady. She was incredibly understanding of Neil, who always wanted to be a vicar.

Once, Neil ordered some cassocks. Mary rang up the supplier and said to them, 'Just tell him they're out of stock' rather than destroy his dream. She was protective of him in a lovely way. She protected him but didn't inhibit him. She was one of the kindest, most lovely people I have ever met. Uncle Harry was very quiet. I remember that he produced his own home brew and had two dogs, Trixie and Prince.

When Neil came to stay he would eat my mum out of house and home. He could almost eat a loaf before a meal.

Neil wanted to run off with the circus – which, as we will see, years later, he did. Paul Bartels remembers:

Once, after Gandey's Circus had been on the Timber Yard, as we called it, Neil went missing. It caused hassle in the village, and PC Ernie Ball and the rest of the police were trying to find him. It turned out he had followed the circus.

Denise also recalls these escapades:

Neil used to try to run away to the circus. When the circus was in town, he would just disappear during the day, but Mary knew where to find him:

at the circus. I don't know where his love of the circus came from.

When they came to Birkenhead, we used to re-enact the circus as kids, and Neil would always be the clown.

NEIL
And Denise was the acrobat.

MALCOLM
Brenda recalls that Neil occasionally had a difficult relationship with his granddad: 'Granddad was a very strict man. He used to expect us all to sit still, but Neil didn't like that. We were quite scared of him, but Neil wasn't.'

Denise remembers that Neil's love of the circus caused problems for the family at Christmas, because Granddad wouldn't have the television on, and the circus was always shown on Christmas Day:

> Granddad always came to our house at Christmas, but he had very fixed views and was very strict. The rest of us just accepted it, but poor Neil couldn't adapt. Granddad insisted that the television should not be watched on Christmas Day and refused to have it on. But Neil was obsessed with the circus, which was always shown on Christmas Day, after *Top of the Pops*, which was on at 2 p.m., and wanted to watch it. He just couldn't understand why the television couldn't be switched on, and kicked up about it. Auntie Mary just tried to shut Neil up.

Normally Mary used to let Neil do whatever he wanted.

Mum and Mary went out once and left Granddad in charge of Neil when he was about six or seven. Neil spent the whole time singing in the bedroom, and Granddad couldn't make him be quiet. Granddad said he could never sleep again in his house because of his bad behaviour.

NEIL

My mum and auntie had gone off to the Battle of Britain celebrations. Granddad told me off for singing in the bedroom and said the bedroom is for sleep, not singing. But I liked my granddad. He'd been in the navy, which is why he had all those rules.

My dad and mum were very good parents. They taught me how to live properly and be nice to people. They looked after me, and they wanted me to be happy, and they took me to Stoke City and the circus and that's why later on I went to Stoke City and the circus.

CHAPTER TWO

NEIL IN THE SIXTIES: A TIME TO SOW

NEIL

When I was fourteen, a student teacher called Dave Cox turned up at my school for a few weeks' teaching practice. He was training to be a teacher at the local university, Keele. He and I got on pretty well, and he said, 'Come along and visit me at Keele.' So I did.

I came on the bus after school. It was March 1960, just after my fourteenth birthday. The campus was all covered in snow – the lawns, the lakes, the woods, everything. It looked marvellous.

I met Dave Cox in the Students' Union. In those days the union was just a Nissen hut. They didn't build the present union building until 1963. I sat down with Dave, we had coffee, then he showed me round, showed me the library and the big old building, Keele Hall, and I thought, I like this, I'll come again. So I arranged with Dave Cox that I would see him next time, and he introduced me to some other students.

.That first time I couldn't get home because of the snow, so Dave Cox invited me to stay. He lived in one of the Nissen huts – lots of the students did in those days; they were left over from the war, with about six students in each one – and they had a spare bed in the hut. I rang my mum and told her where I was. My mum wasn't worried – she always wanted me to be happy.

After that I came to Keele most evenings. By the time Dave Cox left I knew a lot of other people.

It never seemed odd to me. I know that none of my friends from school did anything like going up to Keele and getting to know everyone. But I did. I met the students and the Vice Chancellor, too. You can get things by asking for them. I always do. I got the confidence from my mum, and from the church too.

My mum wasn't worried about me coming to Keele. She wanted me to have a good life. And that's what I've had. She did a good job.

I left school that year. I didn't bother with any exams or anything, and the school didn't put me in for any, so I went to work at Swinnertons. It was a big pottery, and I took the plates to the dip. I did that for about four years. I worked from eight in the morning to five in the afternoon, and then I'd get the bus home and my mum would give me some tea. And then I'd get the bus to Keele and meet my friends there. Saturdays I'd go to the Stoke City match, and Sundays I'd be back at Keele.

MALCOLM

One of the students Neil met in 1961 was Glyn Cherry, a Christadelphian. They are still friends today. Glyn recalls:

I think Neil and I may have first met at a Bible exhibition we held in the Municipal Hall, Newcastle. As a result, Neil came to see me at Keele and came to some of our meetings. One day Neil said, 'My mother wants to meet you.' Two of our Christadelphian members went to see her. It was quite difficult at first because it turned out that Mary was very suspicious and worried about who we were. She was a very devout lady and insisted on saying a prayer at the end of that meeting. But a couple of years later she had a conversion to us and had her Christadelphian baptism. But Neil didn't join us because he doesn't think in terms of religious doctrine at all and likes all the ceremony of the Church of England, which we don't have. Mary was very proud of Neil and always backed him.

The story is typical of Mary. She had a fierce independence of mind, and she also wanted to support Neil's independence, while always keeping an eye on him.

NEIL

We were Church of England but in 1961 I went to a Christadelphian Bible meeting with Glyn Cherry. I told Mum about it and she came with me to a meeting. She liked it so much that she became a Christadelphian but I liked the church and remained C of E. Mum was quite happy about that. She always let me do what I wanted. So long as people believe in God and live a good life it doesn't matter which church they belong to.

One day at the beginning of 1964, I saw Pete Dunkerley in the Students' Union, and I knew he was the new Rag Week Chairman. So I went up to him and I said, 'I want to do the Rag.' And he got me collecting money and made me a marshal, and then he made me Rag Safety Officer. I like Pete Dunkerley. He's a very nice man. And it's a very important job, Rag Safety Officer.

I've been the Rag Safety Officer ever since, and I still am, and Pete and I have been friends ever since. I had to deal with the Rag Committee and the police. I used to go and talk to Sergeant Dave Nixon, and he turned out to be the manager of a police football team, so, when I started the Neil Baldwin Football Club a few years later, we played them.

MALCOLM

Peter Dunkerley (only Neil is allowed to call him Pete these days) is a key figure in Neil's story, because Peter made him a central figure in the annual student Rag, which he's been ever since. In 1964 Peter was an eighteen-year-old undergraduate, the product of a North Manchester grammar school. Peter says:

> The student Rag was a big deal. We had a
> procession half a mile long and we raised a lot of

money for local charities, so it was also a way of putting 'town and gown' together. We needed a lot of willing volunteers, so, when Neil came up to me, the first thing I did was to put a collecting tin in his hand, and he went round with the others to working men's clubs, and came back with a full tin, and he was really pleased at how well he'd done.

For the procession we had to have six marshals – they wore an armband with a big M on them – and I made Neil a marshal and he went and checked on parts of the procession for me, and he really liked doing that. Then one of us – I'm not sure if it was me or Neil – invented the post of Rag Safety Officer for him. He took the job really seriously. He must have done something right: no one was hurt on the procession, then or afterwards.

For the rest of Peter's time at Keele – he left in 1966 – Neil visited his room in one of the student halls of residence about once a week:

> I'd make coffee, he'd talk about what he was doing, about his mother, Stoke City. He was always chatty. Quite often he'd be carrying a Bible but he was never Bible-thumping, he didn't discuss that. He was part of my experience of Keele.

Like many of Neil's oldest friends, Peter has found Neil good at keeping in touch, and gets the occasional visit at his Hampshire home.

19

It was through the Rag that Neil got to know some of the campus children. Keele at that time (and even today to a lesser extent) was unusual because almost all the students and the majority of the lecturers lived on the campus, with lecturers and support staff bringing up their children there. There was a whole community of families, and of course all the campus children loved going to the Rag procession. David Nussbaum's father was a classics lecturer, and David told me:

> One Keele Rag Week in the 1960s, various floats on lorries were parading around, and Neil, of course, was there in the midst of the spectacle. He mentioned that he was 'the safety officer' – which seemed to entail him being able to get on and off any of the floats he wanted to at will, and being given due respect by the students, and of course by us children, as that meant it would be him who decided whether we could get on some of the floats as well.
>
> We campus children of course took Neil as we found him, and rather took to him. He was usually with students, but we sensed he wasn't quite one of them. Indeed, he seemed somehow in charge at times. Neil was also known to me from chapel (where we went on Sunday mornings), so he felt a familiar member of the Keele community. From our perspective as children, students came and went, but Neil seemed always there, from year to year – *with* the students, but not quite one of them.

He started playing football with the campus children. Some of them called him Stan, a reference to the great Stoke City player Stanley Matthews – an ironic reference, as Neil always played football with more enthusiasm than skill.

Those were innocent days. Today, I suppose, the parents would wonder who this strange man was who seemed to enjoy playing with their children, and what his agenda was, and someone would call the police. But I'm glad to say the campus parents in the sixties seemed to take Neil at face value. David's mother, Enid Nussbaum, got to know Neil pretty well. She says:

> After the Keele chapel service one Sunday we invited Neil to lunch. Over lunch, Neil suddenly asked me if we had a telephone. We had. 'Oh,' said Neil, 'I think I'll just phone the Bishop and ask him if I can be ordained.' He was around seventeen, I suppose. I suggested that, as it was Sunday, the Bishop would be very busy – in fact it was highly likely that he wouldn't be at home at all, better to put it off for a day or two, to which suggestion Neil concurred.

In September, 1964, I turned up at Keele, and Neil Baldwin was one of the first people I met.

NEIL

I have been greeting the new students at Keele since I first got to know the campus. I stood just outside the Students' Union – they had the new building by the time Malcolm

21

arrived in 1964. I just came up to the students and said, 'Welcome to Keele. I'm Neil Baldwin.' I did that because I thought it would be nice to meet students and meet people, because in my life I always wanted to meet people. They were OK about it; they liked it, too. Lots of them stopped and had a chat with me.

That's how I met Malcolm. He came along and I said, 'Welcome to Keele. I'm Neil Baldwin.' And he looked quite pleased and he said, 'Thanks. I'm Malcolm Clarke.' And that's how that all started. We've been friends ever since.

Now, I know Malcolm says I was wearing a dog collar, and all I can say to that is, maybe I was. I put it on because I thought it would be nice.

MALCOLM

I was a fresh-faced student of just eighteen. My family had lived at Yarnfield, near Stone, and not far from Stoke, until I was ten, when we moved to York. When I returned to North Staffordshire to come to Keele I was away from home for the first time. I approached the Students' Union nervously. A rotund, jovial figure offered a confident handshake and said, 'Welcome to Keele. I'm Neil Baldwin.' I'm pretty sure he had a dog collar on. I thought he was a few years older than I was – it was some time before I realised we were born in the same year.

I appreciated his warm welcome, but who exactly was he? The university chaplain? I wasn't quite sure. And so it has always been with Neil, who lives by many roles. It is not that he doesn't know the difference between fantasy and reality, but rather that he renders the distinction irrelevant and continually turns one into the other across the loves of his life: Keele University, Stoke City, the Church, circuses, the Boat Race and famous people.

We chatted, and he reminded me that Stoke City were at home a couple of days later. That was how our lifelong friendship started.

NEIL

The job at Swinnertons was all right, but I knew things weren't right and I left in 1964 after four years and went to work at Dewar's butchers in Newcastle-under-Lyme, cutting up meat and serving customers. That was good because it was easier to get to Keele in the evenings, because Newcastle is just down the road from Keele. It's a very short bus ride.

I did it for a year-and-a-half, but it meant I couldn't go to watch Stoke City on Saturdays and I didn't really like the blood, so I went to work at the pottery Woods and Sons. I worked there for fifteen years, right up to 1980. I was a dipper's assistant, and what I did was, I helped the dipper. I helped the dipper check the plates and put them in glaze. It was all right, but towards the end I thought the pottery business was going down.

I'd finish work, go home, have some tea, get the bus up to Keele. On Saturdays I'd go to watch Stoke City, then to Keele, where I'd go to the union bar and the snack bar. On Sundays I'd go to the chapel at Keele. That's where I met the Vice Chancellor, Harold Taylor. He always went to chapel, and Sunday morning I would always meet him. He was an excellent vice chancellor. He was a nice person, he was nice to me. He was a lovely chap. I've known all the vice chancellors since then.

MALCOLM

Harold Taylor was vice chancellor from 1960 to 1967, and, long before he left, his old-fashioned and straitlaced ideas were coming into conflict with the sixties generation of students who were coming to Keele.

One Sunday morning, early in 1965, the BBC came to Keele for the morning service on the radio. It was a big event for Harold Taylor. He was delighted that his university had been chosen, small and new though it was. He was sitting in his place, and, a couple of rows away, there was Neil.

And what neither of them knew was that a student had fixed the wiring, so that, just as some devotional song was beginning, what those in the service and those listening on the radio actually heard was a very loud, raucous pop song, featuring revving motorbike engines, by the Shangri Las, which the BBC had unaccountably banned – the lyric sounds pretty tame now. It was called 'Leader of the Pack'.

NEIL

When 'Leader of the Pack' came on, I was really upset for Harold Taylor. It was the first time he'd appeared in public after his wife died, and it was only two days after Winston Churchill's death. I think it was shocking.

Anyway, he retired two years after that, in 1967, and went to live in Cambridge. I went to see him there, in his retirement. I rang him up and said I was coming. I hitchhiked down there and I went to his house. He remembered me from Keele. That's where I met Mary Glover, who married him after his wife died; she'd been his secretary.

We talked about Keele. He said what a lovely place Keele is, and I said it is. We talked about my work at Keele. And we talked about Princess Margaret, who was the chancellor. I met her at the Students' Union before the Royal Ball one year, and she talked to me again after it. She was the guest of honour. Many years later I performed in front of her as Nello the Clown at a special royal performance of the circus in London.

And another thing happened in 1967, which was marvellous. My friend Malcolm Clarke was elected Students' Union President. That meant he had to dance with Princess Margaret, the university chancellor, at the royal ball – it was one of the things the union president was supposed to do. That was very funny because he can't dance. He's too big and gangly. Our friend Francis Beckett who was also a student calls him 'a man of many parts, clumsily assembled'. Mrs Boote, the Students' Union receptionist, tried to teach him, but she couldn't. I felt sorry for Princess Margaret. I think she got kicked a lot. That's no way to treat the university chancellor.

MALCOLM

It's true. I was advised to keep her in the bar until the formal dance band had gone, so that I didn't have to attempt a waltz. When I finally took her into the ballroom, a jazz band was playing. She said, 'I only do the bunny hop,' and draped her arms round my neck. The problem was that I'm six-foot four and she was small, so she was staring at my navel. I had no idea what a bunny hop was, so I ended up kicking her shins all through that dance. It was the only dance we had all night. Neil wasn't impressed when I told him.

The late 1960s was a very lively time at Keele, as it was at universities throughout the country – indeed, the world. We thought we could change the world by starting with changing the university. The only question was how long it would take us.

Students wanted a much greater involvement in the running of the university and less control by the university over our private lives. Tensions built up throughout my year as president, and, towards the end of my term of office in 1968, I went to the senate to present the students' case. I knew that, if significant concessions were not made, it was likely that the union would decide to take direct action, but the senate gave me very little to take back to the members. A large union meeting was held shortly before the end of term to consider what to do.

I didn't support taking direct action, even though I didn't have any principled objections to it. I just thought it unwise to play our strongest card only a few days before the end of the academic year because the university would just ride out the storm and the threat of direct action would lose much of its potency in the future. I spoke against the motion but it was carried, and the students occupied the registry. I resigned as president because, having opposed the action, I was not the right person to lead the negotiations with the university on the terms on which it would finish. In the end the occupation ended after a couple of days without the university having made any further concessions.

Throughout all this turmoil, Neil simply remained as a constant, dispensing his usual good humour, and continuing to live his life as normal in the Students' Union, and taking an active role in the student Christian community.

They didn't support me over the occupation, but the union general meeting did agree, without any opposition, with my proposal to make Neil Baldwin an honorary life member of the union. And, looking back, I think that was more important than the occupation.

NEIL

They were funny times. I didn't really like the students marching into the registry, and sitting in the registrar's office, but they meant well. I told them that they were being a bit silly but they didn't listen to me – but that's sometimes the trouble with young people: they have to learn.

A few years later things turned more nasty and there was a firebomb thrown at the registrar's house, which was shocking. Once, a few of them took all their clothes off on the roundabout and walked naked into the shop, and it got all over the papers. I didn't like that because it harmed Keele's reputation, and Keele is the best university in the world. Another time they all marched up to the Clock House, where the Vice Chancellor lives, and made a humming noise to try to make it go up in the air. How silly was that!

I'm very pleased that Malcolm made me an honorary life member of the Students' Union and I'm very proud of that. Over the years I've known all the presidents and officers of the union, and some of them have gone on to do wonderful things after leaving Keele. I'm pleased that I helped to set them on their way.

In 1967 I decided to start the Neil Baldwin Football Club, which is still running to this day. I said to some students, 'Would you like to be in my football team?' and everybody thought it was a great idea. The first fixture we had was against a local cement firm. I knew someone who worked there. Then I just started ringing round for fixtures. I just rang up and said, 'This is the Neil Baldwin Football Club. I've got a football team. I'm keen to play you.' That's how it's done. Some of our other early games were against Lincoln Theological College and St John's College, Nottingham. We just turned up to play on the Keele pitches. No one ever said we couldn't.

I have a record of every game we ever played in my flat. We have played 312 games, won 240, drawn twenty-six and lost forty-eight.

I have a lot of connections with Cambridge University. I take the team down to Cambridge quite often to play fixtures against various colleges. We are always given a warm welcome.

MALCOLM

Neil Baldwin Football Club (or NBFC) comprises students of varying levels of footballing ability and is a completely separate team from the university football club. Neil appointed himself as manager, player-manager, coach, kit man and general organiser. I'm not sure that an audit of the playing record would match Neil's official statistics, but nobody is worried about that.

He has appointed a board of directors. I am still on the board, although in over forty years we are still to hold our first meeting.

NEIL

Gary Lineker is the president at the time of writing this. It used to be Kevin Keegan. Gary thinks it is a great honour. We have forty patrons, including former Stoke City manager Lou Macari, Asa Hartford, Joe Corrigan, Gordon Banks, Robbie Fowler, Chic Bates and Peter Shilton. Now it also includes the actor Toby Jones and the rest of the cast of *Marvellous*; Peter, the writer; Julian, the director; Katie, the producer; and Patrick, from the production company Tiger Aspect. Until I gave up playing, I had won Player of the Season over forty times.

MALCOLM

During the 1960s Neil was also a regular outside the Victoria Ground, then Stoke City's ground, and its adjacent training ground, near the middle of Stoke, sometimes teaching his young second cousin, Dan Johnson, the ropes.

In 1967, a young red-haired Irish winger called Terry Conroy came over the water to play for Stoke City. Terry was destined to become an iconic player in Stoke City's history, scoring the first goal at Wembley in 1972 to help secure the League Cup, the only major trophy that Stoke City have ever won. He was a one-club player who has retained his association with the club to this day, being a club ambassador. He has been friends with Neil since his earliest days at Stoke.

Terry went into digs in a terraced house adjacent to the Stoke City ground with another young player called Micky Bloor, just two doors away from George Jackson, another young player. Neil was soon part of their social scene. George remembers:

> Neil would knock on the door and say, 'Can we have a kick-around?' I would sometimes reply, 'I'm having my tea.' But Neil would say, 'Go on' and often as not persuaded me to go out and have a kick-around outside. I've known him ever since then as a friend.

Terry recalls:

> I met Neil during my first week outside the Victoria Ground. He was a big supporter. Fans can become a nuisance but Neil was different. He was funny, but needed looking after. It made me considerate towards him. He was often at the ground. He came into our lodgings and Kate Cope, our landlady, used to feed him.
>
> The football social club across the road had a TV, so we would go in there most evenings. Alf and Ivy Coxon, the landlords, looked after everybody. They put on sandwiches and were very friendly. Some of the other players such as John Mahoney would be there. Everyone knew Neil as 'one of the family'. The people in there took to him and were very protective of him.

We had games of cards and darts but when Neil played darts he would hit everything but the dartboard. There was another lad called Ken Green who used to go in there. He was of limited intelligence, but nobody ever mocked him. We set up darts competitions between Neil and Ken and everybody joined a fan club for one or the other of them. We had to change the rules by abolishing the doubles and make it up to a hundred and not *five* hundred, otherwise the game would never have finished. We even had rosettes with the slogan 'Baldwin for Ever'. Neil would check on everybody's rosette and try and get them to support him, but Ken also had his own supporters' club. There was a big build-up to the darts matches.

George Jackson recalls:

Ken Green worked in the railways. Neil and Ken always had a rivalry, so we organised a darts competition and on one occasion they both dressed up as professional boxers with boxing shorts and gloves. Throwing the darts wearing boxing gloves was hilarious, with people shouting for one or the other, but we turned it into an occasion to raise money for charity. Neil has always been willing to do anything to raise money for good causes.

Terry says:

> We would also create little scenarios to keep us entertained. At that time there was a lot of trouble at football matches and we would re-enact little scenes where Neil would be the Stoke supporter, George Jackson and Terry Lees would pretend to be opposition supporters and bump into him and soon Neil would be on the floor. Neil would then say, 'Let's do it the other way round.' But, whichever way round it was done, Neil never won. Of course, it was all in good spirits.

George:

> Sometimes we would go round to Terry's at Number 4 and say, 'What should we do?' We'd agree to re-enact something. Me and Neil would be the Stoke players. For example, we'd pretend that Stoke had won five–nil, that Neil had scored a hat-trick and that hooligans were causing trouble. Terry and Micky would pretend to be one of the hooligans. Terry would say, 'You two play for Stoke, we'll get you.' The plan was that we get duffed up. Sometimes we would swap round so that Neil was the hooligan, but he always still ended up on the bottom.

On one occasion the entertainment was more formal. Here's Terry again:

For Christmas 1970 we decided to do a pantomime. On Sundays the club closed at 2 p.m. and we would rehearse after that. We decided to do *Cinderella* about six weeks before Christmas. We would be constantly rewriting the script.

We realised that we had to find parts for Neil and Ken Green. We decided that Neil would be Prince Barmcake. I was an Ugly Sister. John Mahoney was Buttons. I've still got the script at home.

NEIL

I was Prince Charming. Terry was the Barmcake.

MALCOLM

Terry continues:

> Neil came out from backstage with only one line to say. He always wagged his finger in the air which itself reduced the audience to hysterics. His line was, 'I suppose you know why I am here.' But Neil always said 'suspose' instead of 'suppose'. We tried to teach him to say 'suppose' instead of 'suspose' but without success. He would come to the rehearsal, put his finger up again and say, 'I suspose you know why I am here.' We tried for three weeks to get it right, but on the final Sunday we decided that it was funnier to leave it in. The club was packed. It was a success beyond our wildest dreams and hilariously funny. Everybody agreed that Neil was the star of the show.

George also recalls the pantomime: 'Neil was in it as Prince Charming. It filled the club, his line was, "I suppose you know why I am here." But he couldn't say "suppose". It brought the house down.'

George also recalls how Neil harboured his own hopes of becoming a footballer:

> One time Neil said he wanted a trial, so we decided to organise a trial. We took him on the far side of the training ground to have a warm-up. Neil was shattered even after the warm-up, so we never got as far as the trial.
>
> On one occasion Neil announced to our astonishment that he had got a trial at Exeter City. When he came back we said, 'How have you got on?' All we could get out of him was a complaint that Exeter City wouldn't pay his expenses and he had to thumb it back.

NEIL

George has got that wrong. It wasn't Exeter. It was Blackpool. I got locked in the dressing room. They forgot I was there. I also had a trial at Crewe Alexander when Alan A'Court was in charge there.

MALCOLM

George continues:

> Neil used to clean cars for the players to raise a bit of money. One time Terry Lees decided to pull

Neil's leg by pretending he wasn't satisfied and saying, 'I'm not paying you, you haven't done it right.' Neil was horrified and challenged him to a fight. Terry said, 'Take your jumper off' and pretended to accept the challenge, but of course he wasn't serious. All the lads loved Neil. He was part of the scenery.

We never let anybody take things too far, but Neil had a lot of spirit and always gave something back. He made quite an impression on my life.

We were once driving past Keele in Dave Hughes's car. It was pouring down at half past midnight and we spotted someone walking down Keele Bank to Newcastle town centre. It was Neil. We asked him where he was going and Neil just replied, 'You're taking me where I'm going!' Dave had a mannequin from the Just Jane dress shop in the back, so he sat Neil in the back with a naked woman. They were an interesting pair of passengers.

The former Stoke player John Ruggiero recounts the time when the famous England international George Eastham signed for Stoke. George had been in England's 1966 winning World Cup squad and some years later was to score the winning goal for Stoke in the 1972 League Cup final at Wembley. He now lives in South Africa. John recounts the tale as told to him by George:

When George signed for Stoke City, the club put him in a house in Sneyd Green. He'd been there a few days when there was a knock on the door and he opened it to see a vicar standing on the doorstep. George thought, I've only been here a week and they've sent the local vicar round to make sure I'm all right and settling into the local community.

He really appreciated this gesture and invited the vicar in for tea. George produced some tea and biscuits and then noticed that the vicar had taken out large number of books and magazines and asked George to start signing them. George thought this was very odd. Eventually, he discovered that it was Neil, not a real vicar. He took a great deal of ribbing from the other players about that, but George has a great deal of time for Neil and, whenever he rings up from South Africa, always asks, 'How's Nello?'

George was neither the first nor the last to be taken in by Neil's occasional dog collar. I had done the same on my first meeting with Neil a couple of years earlier at Keele University. In those days Neil also occasionally used to wear it while hitchhiking.

NEIL

I used to hitchhike to visit old Keele friends, circuses, church services and football matches. I found that wearing a dog collar was a very good way of getting a quick lift, because drivers liked to pick up someone in the church. My ministry's very important to me. In those days, all the students used to hitchhike, but nobody does any more. I haven't been hitchhiking for a long time. I find it's better to just to ask friends for a lift.

MALCOLM

Betty Cartwright, a longstanding member of St Mark's church in Birkenhead, which Mary and Neil used to attend when visiting her family, recalls an incident in the late sixties or early seventies:

> Neil wore a dog collar, which led our minister, Canon Maurice Marshall, to believe he was a vicar and he invited him back to the church to preach at a later date. The family had to go round to tell Maurice the truth.

Denise recalls her mother Iris saying, 'I just can't believe our Neil has fooled Maurice.'

Cousin Brenda confirmed that Maurice was a 'rather stiff' person who wasn't too pleased that he had been misled in this way.

It was during the sixties that Neil started to turn his childhood interest in circuses into an adult reality. Norman Barrett MBE is one of the circus community's most famous members, a ringmaster and former bareback rider who is also famous for his act with trained budgies. Norman recalls:

> I first got to know Neil in the 1960s. He came to visit my mother, who invited him for a cup of tea and gave him some circus programmes. And

he became a regular visitor after that. On one occasion he came with a dog collar and a Bible. He came to see us at the Tower Circus in Blackpool, and also to Zippos in Stoke and down to shows in London.

He took my retired budgies and I still give him budgies because he takes great care of them.

He's a circus lover; he visits circuses all over the country, and indeed the world. He goes to the annual get-together of the circus community and the circus fans' association. He still phones me regularly.

Phillip Gandey of Gandey's Circus says, 'Neil used to visit my father's circus as a young man and always visited my mum and dad. We see him at family funerals and know him as a friend. He is part of the wider circus family.'

Andrew Edwards is a local funeral director with strong connections to Stoke City. He recalls:

A few years ago, we did the funeral of Mary Gandey, who was prominent in the circus community. Mourners came from all over the country. I was very surprised to see Nello there, but I shouldn't have been, because it was obvious he's a friend of the family and knew loads of people from the circus families very well.

NEIL

Norman and Phillip are very good friends of mine. Norman is one of the most famous circus people and has one of the best acts in the country. I have been pleased to look after his retired budgies. I have known Phillip's family ever since I was young, and in 1974 I performed in a show of theirs at Stoke Polytechnic as a clown. All the Gandey family are good friends of mine. I went to Mary's funeral at Brereton. That was sad. It was organised by Andrew Edwards, who is a big Stoke City fan. He is a nice man who is very good at running funerals.

I see a lot of my old circus friends at the annual national circus reunion. A circus is the most exciting form of entertainment you can have. I love making people laugh.

CHAPTER THREE

NEIL IN THE SEVENTIES: POLITICS, FOOTBALL AND THE BOAT RACE

NEIL

I've always been a big Labour Party supporter, so I was very pleased when, in 1971, my friend Malcolm Clarke was elected to Newcastle Borough Council as Labour councillor for May Bank, and even more pleased when they made him mayor three years later, on 1 April 1974. He was only twenty-seven. That's very young to be mayor. I think he was the youngest mayor Newcastle has ever had.

I was the first person to ride in the mayor's car that year, which was marvellous. I was really pleased that Malcolm and his wife Lesley became mayor and mayoress. They were very good at it, and I went to their Mayor's and Mayoress's Balls. Lots of mayors and lord mayors have been very good friends of mine. I think Malcolm knows by now that, if I say I know someone famous, I do.

Of course, he nearly lost it again the day after he got it, due to some sort of carry-on. I went to the public gallery to cheer him on.

MALCOLM

It's a long story but, having been elected mayor on 1 April, due to reorganisation I had to resign on 2 April and they had to run the election again on 3 April. So my first term of office lasted just one day, All Fools' Day, which somehow seemed appropriate.

Bizarrely, and somewhat embarrassingly, the only civic engagement on that day was the university's annual dinner for its friends and neighbours, so I returned to where I worked for that, knowing that it might need only one comrade to miss a bus to the meeting on 3 April for it to be my one and only civic engagement. Neil, of course, turned up at the dinner.

The next day, with Neil watching anxiously from the public gallery, on 3 April I was elected for my second term of office. After the meeting, we had to adjourn to the Clayton Lodge hotel for a civic reception. This involved a journey in the mayor's Daimler.

Neil came up to me outside. 'Can I have ride in the mayor's car?'

'Of course, Neil.'

I was immediately made aware that this course of action wasn't recommended by the Mayor's Sergeant. It was the first, but certainly not the last, decision about how I conducted myself as mayor that wasn't in accord with the traditional way of doing things. One of these was giving hitchhiking students a lift in the mayor's car up Keele bank when I was returning to work after an engagement.

So, anyway, Neil climbed into the car, and, as we glided away, he began to give a royal wave through the window to bemused bystanders and pedestrians.

Neil was never shy about giving me advice on what the council should be doing.

As mayor, I went to a function at which some of the Stoke City players were present, and had a chat with the winger Terry Conroy. The conversation turned to Neil and I remarked, 'I sometimes wondered whether Neil really knew the Stoke City players quite as well as he said he did.'

'That's funny,' Terry replied, 'because we were doubtful whether he really knew the Mayor of Newcastle.'

NEIL

As well as helping Malcolm with his mayoral duties, I carried on going to Keele, and at the start of the seventies I got to know some very nice people there who were in the Christian Union. There was Jonathan Gledhill, who's a very nice man and is the Bishop of Lichfield, but announced in March 2015 that he would retire the following September; and there were Tony Andrews, Vic Trigg and Tony Bartlett, and they're all still very good friends of mine.

MALCOLM

Tony Andrews remembers:

> After a while, Neil began sleeping on my floor every weekend. I would have what I called the Neil

Baldwin kit in the corner. Jonathan Gledhill was a year above me and also lived in my block. Vic Trigg and Tony Bartlett came later. We looked after Neil and kept an eye on him. His mother, Mary, used to take us for an occasional meal as a reward.

Vic Trigg recalls his first meeting with Neil a few days after arriving in Keele in 1972:

I was offered a coffee by a final-year student, Tony Andrews, who lived on my corridor, and amongst the eight or so people already in Tony's room was a slightly dishevelled and portly figure sitting on the edge of the desk looking benevolently down on the students who were sitting on the bed, chairs and floor. I was introduced to the twenty-six-year-old Neil, but no explanation as to his reason for being there was given, and I took him for some sort of social worker or perhaps a chaplaincy assistant.

Over the next few weeks I noticed that Neil's mum drove him up to Keele every Friday night with a sleeping bag and camp bed and he then slept on Tony's floor for two nights and was collected by his mum on Sunday evenings. Tony was a little vague as to Neil's exact role beyond what I picked up myself, that he spent his weekends talking to students, drinking coffee and consuming any food that was offered. He also went to every Stoke City home match and mixed with the university staff and chaplains. I discovered that Neil had a job as a labourer in Woods Pottery in Burslem during the week and that he had already been coming up to Keele for more than a decade. He was also very interested in anything to do with the Church of England and its clergy, circuses and the university boat race, exclusively relating to the Cambridge crew.

As I had a car, I often provided a taxi service to Neil and that has been continuing ever since.

Neil's dad died during the first term I was at Keele. Tony Andrews was a big support for his mum at this time as she learned how to pay bills, complete forms, get the car serviced, that sort of thing, and it was at this time that I first got to know Mary.

NEIL

My dad died from gall-bladder cancer. The doctor told us he wouldn't last until Christmas, and he didn't. It upset me because he was in a lot of pain and there was nothing I could do about it. Vic and the two Tonys were very good friends to me and Mum at that time and have been ever since.

They are all very good friends of mine. I've known Bishop Jonathan since he was a lad. I always thought he would become a bishop, and he's a very good one. He took the service of thanksgiving for my fifty years at Keele in 2010.

Tony Andrews is another very good friend. I used to sleep on his floor, and his cups of coffee were very good. He has often put me up when I visit London. A few years ago he found a very good German hotel for me in Putney, where I stay when I go down for the Boat Race. They like me there, and I like them. They do very good breakfasts.

Tony Bartlett and his wife, Irene, invite me to Christmas Day lunch every year. We always watch the Queen's message. Vic and Helen have been very good to me. Before she died, my mum asked them to look after my money, which they do. My mum used to have her caravan in their garden at Market Drayton. Tony and Vic built the aviary for my birds in the flat.

MALCOLM
Tony Bartlett remembers:

> Vic was the first person I met in Horwood B block in 1972 and we've been mates ever since. I went to Keele as a Roman Catholic, Vic was Pentecostal and he soon introduced me to Neil, who was involved with the church.
>
> Vic had a car and used to give Neil lifts, so we often saw Neil and his mum Mary during my early years at Keele. Mary was very accommodating. She was also astute, calm and clear. She would be very proud, but slightly worried, by everything which is going on for Neil now. She lived her faith and did things for people.
>
> After graduating I stayed on as a resident tutor in a block at Keele. Mary used to call in to see me. She took us out for trips. But her driving was pretty poor. I always felt closer to heaven when being a passenger with Mary driving.

Mary's poor driving was legendary. Tony wasn't the only one to have his nerves tested. We have already heard young Dan's memory of it on the trips to the safari park. Vic says, 'Mary was a terrible driver. She once knocked a paper-boy off his bike, burned out clutches regularly and drove very slowly at the head of queues.'

Today, Vic works as a part-time driving instructor. Tony Bartlett muses, 'I've often wondered whether Vic's decision to train to become a driving instructor was motivated by his memory of Mary's driving.'

These friends have remained in contact with Neil ever since and have helped him on many occasions. Vic says:

> After Tony Andrews graduated I took on the role of host to Neil each weekend and, unless there was a spare room somewhere, Neil slept on my floor during term time on most weekends for the next three years.
>
> One year Mary and Neil had a holiday at my parents' home on the south coast, and my parents stayed with Mary in her prefab in Chesterton when they came to my graduation in 1976.

Tony Bartlett's parents also hosted a holiday for Neil and Mary: 'In 1976–7 Neil and Mary came up to Thornaby-on-Tees and stayed with my mum and dad. They visited places like Whitby.'

But not everything they did gained Neil's support. Tony recalls:

Neil didn't approve of myself, Roger Bachelor and John Hughes climbing the chapel one year to put a 'Jesus Saves' sign on the roof. Vic remained at the bottom pretending to be drunk. Neil really didn't like the idea of us doing something stupid – no doubt this fitted in with his role as Rag Safety Officer.

Bishop Jonathan Gledhill says:

My first memory of Neil is of him organising a football match at Keele between his football team and the Christian Union. He has kept in touch ever since those days. He rings me about once a year, usually either on my birthday or at Christmas and is always very courteous. He always has a view on who's likely to get which job when in the Church, and, to my amazement and occasional annoyance, he's very often right. I think he keeps up to date by ringing lots of people. I've often seen him in his morning suit in St Paul's cathedral or just sitting at the back in the service for the ordination of a new vicar at a parish. It would be a great pity if the churches didn't want to embrace eccentrics like Neil.

NEIL

I always knew Jonathan would make bishop one day. I know most of the bishops and I get them all to sign the order of service when I go a bishop's consecration.

In 1973, my mum and I took a holiday on the south coast with Vic and his parents. On the way down we stopped in Oxford and I went into a theological college to talk about training for the ministry. I always wanted to be a vicar and went to talk to them about it, but it came to nothing.

Then on the way back we stopped in Oxford again and I saw the Duke of Edinburgh. I think he was doing something for his Awards. I said to Mum, 'I must go over and speak to him.' She said, 'Don't, Neil, because of all this trouble with the IRA.' But it's not every day a member of the royal family has a chance to speak to me, so I crossed the road to let him have a word with me. We talked about world problems. He was very pleased to listen to my advice. He was a very nice man.

About that time I managed to have a talk with Harold Wilson too, when he was prime minister. We were in London for the Rag and went to Downing Street. In those days there wasn't a fence across the end of the road, like there is now, and you could walk right down it, so we did. I said I wanted to sell a Rag magazine to the Prime Minister. They let me knock on the door and I saw Harold Wilson, who bought a magazine.

I was quite lucky he was in. He was a very nice man. I told him that it was good that a Labour man is Prime Minister, and gave him some advice about what to do. I don't think they would let even me do that these days. Did you know his wife's name was Mary Baldwin before she married him, the same as my mum's? All the Baldwins are good people.

MALCOLM

Neil also continued his friendship with campus families and their children. Godfrey Jordan, whose father was a maths lecturer, and Chris Tough, son of the deputy registrar, remember the football games. Godfrey says:

> Chris and I have memories from the early to mid-seventies, when we were eleven to fourteen years old. We and our pals were the 'campus kids', sons and daughters of the academic and administrative staff and residents on Keele campus. Our parents had fought hard with the Keele authorities to get us a space to play football and cricket on what became known as the 'top field' near the houses on the campus where we lived.
>
> We were kids rather than the young adults involved in Neil Baldwin FC. The main memory is the unexpected arrival of Neil at our football games on the top field, where he would turn up with several others and cheerfully join in our game. I never worked out quite why a group of men dressed in Stoke City shirts would be wandering around Keele looking for a game. Mystifyingly they turned up from the Newcastle side of the top field, not the university side. Presumably, they'd walked up from the Westlands or Silverdale.
>
> There was a seriousness and intensity about the game when he joined. Names of current Stoke players were assigned to each of us – you had no choice: Neil would simply allocate a name – and the

scoring of a goal was followed with handshakes all round. I recall Neil's intense level of encouragement and shouting as we were playing. I also vaguely remember them disappearing almost as abruptly as they arrived and wondering where on earth they came from and where they were going.

The other memory is of course his semi-permanent presence on the campus. Frequently wearing a long university scarf, he was ubiquitous and would shout a cheery hello – sometimes disconcertingly cheerful.

Peter Whieldon was the son of Harold and Margaret Whieldon, caretakers in Horwood Hall. Harold was also a church warden at St John's Church in Keele village. Harold and Margaret were much-loved figures among the students. Peter recalls:

I always thought Neil was a student. We used to play football on Horwood Green until Doc Henderson, the warden, chased us off, and when this happened I have vivid recollections of Neil's back disappearing into 'A' block.

Sometimes he used to come into our bungalow, where my mum would feed him, as she did everybody.

During the Rag I was sometimes put in the lead vehicle and Neil used to run around all over the place as the safety officer.

Occasionally he used to do lay reading in the

village church for Harold. I can still remember Neil's first reading in the early seventies. He was wearing a blue lay-reader's vestment.

NEIL

I have taught a lot of the campus children how to play football. I'm a very good coach. They have to learn that you don't win football matches if you don't score goals. This is what I tell the NBFC players.

I am always willing to preach or read at other churches, and I'm a very good lay reader. Harold Whieldon was a very good friend of mine and a keen Christian. He looked after St John's for many years. I was sad when his wife Margaret died of cancer in 1982. She was a lovely lady who looked after me and the students very well. There is a plaque in her memory in the row of trees on the university land right opposite the church.

Of course, I didn't neglect the Neil Baldwin Football Club. It went from strength to strength in the seventies.

MALCOLM

Linden West, now a professor at Christchurch University, Kent, played in the NBFC and remembers an away game at Oxford University in the early 1970s:

> We all went down on the coach to Oxford and we were made very welcome with a very posh lunch. When the match started it soon became apparent that the teams were hopelessly unbalanced and they were far better than us. I think the match

Wearing a replica 1972 Stoke City League Cup winner's shirt signed by members of the winning team.

Left: Enjoying a sunny day in Neil's grandparents' garden with Uncle Morris and his cousin Brenda.

Right: Mary and Aunt Iris with Neil and Brenda in one of Neil's favourite spots: outside a circus in New Brighton.

Above: A young Neil with his family at Aunt Iris's wedding.

Above: Neil almost takes centre-stage at another happy family event – cousin Denise's wedding.

Left: Mary, wearing a Keele scarf, with Helen Trigg on the boat race launch in 1977.

Right: Mary with close friends Helen, Irene and Vic in 1975.

Above left: Mary with Neil, wearing Malcolm's PhD robes in 1977. Nowadays, Neil can wear his own Keele robes.

Above right: Mary with her beloved dog, Jessie.

Below: Neil with Jessie outside Mary's caravan.

Left: A reflective Nello between performances.

Right: Nello and Malcolm in 1981, with daughters Zara and Zoe, outside Neil's caravan.

Left: Neil visiting Swiss circus KNIE in 2006.

Above: Antics in the dressing room, years before Neil was the kit man: Nello tries to cheer up manager Alan Durban and the players (Jeff Cook, Ray Evans, Peter Hampton and Paul Bracewell).

Below: 'Lord Baldwin' with Lou (*front right*), Winnie and Chic Bates (*at rear*), and players (*left to right*) Tony Kelly, Vince Overson, Lee Sandford, Dave Regis, Carl Beeston and Kevin Russell.

Inset: The business card says it all!

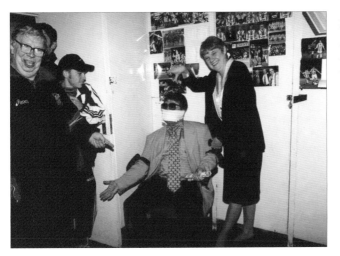

Left: Neil and Winnie kidnap George Andrews, who was meant to be on air.

Right: Neil at home in the laundry at the Victoria Ground.

Left: Neil and the party enjoy a drink in Venice before the Anglo-Italian cup game.

Above: Neil – wearing Lou's top – with the Stoke City youth team in France.

Below left: Neil in his Ninja Turtle outfit at Leyton with his friend the late Jonathan Macari.

Below right: The 'chicken' at Bournemouth with a bemused Malcolm and Zara in the background.

might actually have been against the Oxford University Football Club first team and they may have thought they were playing the Keele first team. I think we were about five goals down in the first twenty minutes.

After one of the goals I remember getting told off by the manager, Neil, for not marking my man properly. He was running, or rather walking, around with his fist clenched, telling us all to 'get a grip'. I think the match was also delayed a few times because Neil had trouble keeping his shorts up. The rest of us found it rather difficult to take this on-field humiliation as seriously as the captain was doing.

NEIL

Linden has not got too much to shout about. Some of the goals were his fault. We didn't play very well that day. As I kept telling the team, you can't win football matches if you let goals in like that. They also say I forgot to collect the coach fares, which meant my mum getting quite a big bill, and I think I did. But it was a great day nevertheless.

MALCOLM

It may have been as a result of the coach bill that Mary decided that sometimes she needed to keep a much closer eye on the things Neil was organising. She also used to worry about his birthday parties and other events because sometimes the room hire might not be paid. She wanted to see what financial commitments Neil was entering into, because she was the one who had to pick up the bill. As a result she decided she needed to read some of his letters, but felt guilty about doing this, so she invited the local vicar round to steam them open, because she felt this somehow made it legitimate.

Meanwhile, Neil continued his support for Stoke City. On one occasion in November 1975 Stoke City were playing away at Queens Park Rangers (QPR). My wife Lesley and I had arranged to go to the game and spend the weekend in London with friends. Neil asked me, 'Are you going down for the game at the weekend?'

'Yes, we're going down to London on Friday night and making a weekend of it.'

'Will you give me a lift down?'

'Of course.'

'Can you pick me up from work?' Neil was working at Woods Pottery.

'Of course.'

So we went first in the wrong direction to pick up Neil from Woods at the end of his working day before setting off to London.

'Where are you staying, Neil?'

He told us he was staying with a former Keele friend. I'm not sure, but it could well have been Tony Andrews, who was Neil's main source of a London bed. It was somewhere well to the west side of London, a very large detour for us.

'How are you getting out there, Neil?'

'Can you drop me off there?' We couldn't say no and leave him to navigate the London transport system on his own. The only option was to drop him off at the address to make sure that he would be all right.

'Of course, Neil. What time is he expecting you?'

'I haven't arranged a time.'

'He does know you're coming, doesn't he, Neil?'

'Er, no, but he won't mind me coming to stay.'

'But what if he's not there, Neil? Suppose he's gone away for the weekend or something.'

This possibility had not entered Neil's mind but it didn't seem to worry him. However, we began to worry about what Neil would do if he wasn't there. We knew that the friends we were staying with hadn't got any spare room.

We drew up outside the house and Neil walked up the path. I waited to make sure that somebody was there. We saw the door opened by Neil's would-be host, and noted the surprised look on his face when he saw Neil unexpectedly on his doorstep. We decided not to hang around.

When I next saw Neil, I learned that, after a fine breakfast, his host had kindly given him a lift to QPR's Loftus Road ground before the game. Neil had waited outside the players' entrance, as was his wont, and, inevitably, been given a complimentary ticket by one of the players.

After the game, which Stoke lost, he somehow managed to blag a lift back on the team coach, where I imagine he shared the players' tea. After arriving back at the Victoria Ground, the late Ian Moores, one of the Stoke players, who scored that day, and who lived in Silverdale, diverted via Keele on his route home to drop Neil off.

So Neil was back in the Keele Students' Union by about 9.30 p.m. on Saturday, having left work at 5 p.m. the night before, gone to the game and, as far as I can see, hadn't spent a penny in the process. Not a lot of people have ever done that.

NEIL

I started getting interested in the Boat Race through watching it on TV, so I decided to go down there. I stayed with Tony Andrews. I have always been a big Cambridge supporter. I used to go from the Thursday to the Saturday of the race and got to know everybody, including all the crew.

I got to know Alf, who was in charge of the boats, and went round to his house. He was a very good friend of mine. He got me an invitation to go on the official Cambridge launch. I also got invited to the Boat Race Ball, which used to be at the Savoy Hotel.

MALCOLM

How on earth did he do that? I don't know. But one of the things I know he did was to write fan letters to members of the crew. It must have been heart-warming to get a letter out of the blue saying what a great oarsman you are. Some of the rowers were from other countries, particularly the USA, and probably didn't have family here, which perhaps made it easier to give Neil an invitation to the launch or the ball.

I can remember him telling me that he was going on an official launch in March sometime in the seventies. To be honest, I thought it was a bit of Neil exaggeration, but soon realised it probably wasn't when I saw him on TV. If Neil tells you he's going to do something, it's rarely wise to dismiss it, however unlikely it seems.

Steve Russell also saw Neil on television in 1975. Steve arrived at Keele the previous September and was to become another of Neil's friends and admirers:

> I had heard of a character who went around the student flats drinking coffee and borrowing books, which he then exchanged with the next student. I was a fresher and went to the sports centre to see if there was any rowing, but no luck. On my way back I struck up a conversation with what I assumed was a fellow student, who informed me that he went to the Oxford and Cambridge Boat Race every year and was very interested in rowing. I later found out the person I had been speaking to was Neil Baldwin and was told not to pay attention to whatever he said.
>
> In March I was at home settling down to watch the Boat Race on telly. There used to be a special [TV sports programme] *Grandstand* on then that covered it all afternoon. Watching Frank Bough interviewing on the towpath, I saw a familiar face trying to get his attention to be interviewed – Neil Baldwin. I always believed everything he said after that.

Not only did Neil go on the launch, but he invited guests to go with him. Vic Trigg recalls:

> In 1977 and 1978 Helen and I were honoured to go on the official Cambridge launch. Tony Andrews

was also there in 1977 and Neil's mum Mary was there too. Both universities had a launch, which were like pleasure boats and followed the crews. We have got a photograph of Mary on the launch wearing a Keele scarf.

Chris Ballieu was president of the Cambridge University Boat Club in 1973, having been given his first 'blue' in 1970, and has been Neil's contact for the Boat Race ever since that time:

I live in Putney, so I keep in contact with the boat club and the crew at the Boat Race each year. I always know first hand what's going on. I think that's why Neil always rings me to tell me when he's coming down. What he really wants is a chance to have a word with the crew, although this is not always easy to arrange because they're kept apart in the days before the race. It's a matter for the president, not me, and of course there's a different president each year.

He doesn't have a formal arrangement with the boat club, but has stayed in contact with me all these years. He's a fixture. He's Cambridge's most loyal supporter. Information about Neil gets passed by word of mouth each year. When he comes he always asks after other crew members from the past, for example, David Mitchell, who was a crew member in 1971. Neil took a particular shine to him and still asks after him. He also asks after Ben

Duncan, who was in the crew in 1973, and was president the following year.

I can't recall exactly what happened about Neil going on the Cambridge launch. Nowadays there are strict regulations that won't allow more than twelve people on the Cambridge launch on the Boat Race day, and it's very difficult to get onto it. For example, there's a ballot among former Blues for a single place. They can take more passengers than that, but are not currently allowed to. So I don't think even Neil with all his persuasive powers could get on it today, but I think these more restrictive rules weren't introduced until the 1980s.

Although there's a separate umpire's launch these days, back in the 1970s the umpire travelled on one of the university's launches, alternating each year between Oxford and Cambridge. The umpire would be provided by one of the boat clubs, but would undertake his duties from the launch of the other one. I think it was in the 1980s that the umpire's boat was introduced. So it's quite possible that he was on the same launch as the umpire.

There used to be a Boat Race Ball, but that died the death round about 1971 or 1972. A different type of ball was recreated by myself and others in 1973–74 and it lasted for about ten years. It's quite possible that Neil attended one or more of these balls. If Neil thinks that one of them was held at the Savoy Hotel he might well be right.

Back to the Neil Baldwin Football Club, and Steve Russell recalls an internal NBFC game in the late 1970s and the sighting of another famous sporting personality:

> In my final year at Keele, 1977–78, I was involved in a football match arranged by Neil. I was drinking in the bar when I became aware of an animated discussion between Neil and some residents of D Block. They'd been bragging that they could beat any team that Neil could get together. Having been recently beaten by them in a five-a-side match, playing for E Block, which was settled by a disputed penalty, I agreed to play for Neil's team whenever called to do so.
>
> Several weeks later, on a Sunday morning after a heavy night, there came a knock on my door. It was Neil with his kit, waking me up to play in the game.
>
> At the sports centre, the changing rooms for home and away had a communal shower, which you could walk through. In one changing room were Neil and me and in the other a full team. Neil went out for a minute and to my astonishment returned informing me that Geoff Hurst, who scored a hat-trick in the World Cup final, was in the corridor. I knew that Geoff Hurst had played for Stoke City and ran a local pub. I went out and was relieved to see Geoff Hurst in cricket whites, not football kit!
>
> Venturing onto the field of play, I was surprised

to see an old neighbour of mine, Kev Brennan, the captain of the first team at Keele. He informed me that they were to play with Neil, that the goalkeeper was going to be late and could I take his place?

At kick-off, Kev reassured me that I wouldn't have anything to do. The next thing I did was pick the ball out of the net. 'Right,' said Kev, 'that's it – no mercy!'

From then on Neil's team dominated the game. D Block never touched the ball and every chance was set up for Neil to score. He got about three or four goals. He was presented with a trophy for 'Man of the Match' by his mum and an ex-Stoke and England player.

NEIL

Steve hasn't got that story right. It was F Block we played, and we won 8–4. We played them two years in a row and I scored in both games. I always score.

Steve Benn used to play for the NBFC, too. He was the son of the then Labour cabinet minister Tony Benn and he was at Keele in the early seventies.

So, on one of my trips to London in the mid-seventies, I went to the House of Commons and sent in a 'green card' for Tony Benn with the message, 'Neil Baldwin from Keele, friend of Steve's.' Tony Benn came out to see me and naturally took me for a meal in the Commons restaurant.

MALCOLM

He certainly did. I heard about this from the late John Golding, who was the MP for Newcastle-under-Lyme at the time and also a Keele graduate, so naturally he knew Neil, who was one of his more colourful constituents and a strong Labour supporter.

John Golding also hated Tony Benn – Golding was the fixer for Labour's right wing, and Benn the leader of the left.

John used to tell the tale of arriving at the restaurant and being astonished to see Her Majesty's Secretary of State for Energy dining with Neil Baldwin. He didn't know about the Steve connection and was mystified as to how this could possibly have come about. He waited at the door feasting his eyes on this extraordinary scene for as long as he dare before departing because he didn't want to be spotted by Neil and called over.

Stephen Benn had met Neil Baldwin in his first year at Keele, which was 1969–70:

> I suppose I came across him in the same way that so many people did – he was just there. I might have first talked to him outside or inside the Students' Union building. He was very welcoming and, while it was clear from the beginning that he wasn't a student, he seemed to be a permanent fixture. He was always friendly and unfailingly courteous. He never seemed to take offence and I was one of those (and there were many) who talked to him whenever we came across him. He always seemed to call me 'Steve', though no one else did.

I suppose I ought to add that some (though only a few) students in my year disparaged him and thought him 'strange' and 'simple' and they would sometimes poke fun at him. But I never did and the more I got to know him the more genuine he seemed. He had no 'side' at all and he was always friendly and open, and you just sort of got to know him as he was – because that's who he was.

I used to play a fair amount of football and that's how I first came across the Neil Baldwin Football Club. I need hardly add that the president was Neil Baldwin. He organised some games and I was invited to play.

He would be the first to admit that he wasn't fast and would have trouble keeping up with a game. Often, people wouldn't pass to him, yet he was always there running as best he could up and down the pitch. But the point was that he enjoyed it and it was his team and he made it all possible.

Apart from being president, there was one other privilege that he always exercised. It was Neil who took the penalties. I remember in one game a penalty had been awarded and Neil duly stepped forward to take it. However, he didn't strike it hard enough and the goalkeeper didn't have much difficulty in saving it – indeed, he couldn't avoid saving it. But the referee whistled for a retake and Neil had a second chance. This time he hit it better and I think the goalkeeper made an exaggerated attempt to save it by diving over the ball. Neil had scored his goal and he positively beamed with pleasure. It was a moment like that when you couldn't help but be a proud participant in the game.

I also came to realise that he never made anything up. When he said that such-and-such was going to happen it invariably did.

On another occasion the NBFC was playing a 'home' game at the Keele [University] Sports Centre and Neil had announced in advance that we were going to play in Stoke City football kit. There were a few doubters, followed by looks of amazement when we got to the game to find Neil handing out real Stoke City football shirts. It was amazing.

I'm not sure exactly when Neil met my dad. Certainly my dad came to speak at Keele in 1970 – and addressed a packed auditorium – so I wouldn't rule out the possibility that he just went up to him and said hello, as he did with so many people. Perhaps Neil was around my graduation ceremony in 1973, when both my parents were there, and simply came up and introduced himself. However, it might equally be the case that they hadn't met at all – not until Neil showed up at the House of Commons in the later 1970s.

Neil arrived at the House of Commons one evening – in those days there wasn't the security system in place that there is now – and just walked in through St Stephen's entrance and up into Central Lobby. There he went to the desk and put in a 'green card' for Tony Benn MP. He was then in the cabinet. My dad was in the House and came out to meet him. Neil explained that he was 'a friend of Steve's' and on that basis alone my dad took him in and they had a talk. It was typical of my dad that he should have done this and devoted some time to someone that he quite possibly had not met before.

The fact that this incident occurred was only known publicly because the local MP for Newcastle-under-Lyme, John Golding MP, noticed Neil and my dad together and doubtless wondered how it had come about.

My dad phoned me later to report what had happened and said he'd met a 'friend of yours', though I could tell by his voice that he hadn't been sure that he was a student in my year – but I explained that I did indeed know Neil and I thanked him for having made Neil welcome.

NEIL

Tony Benn was very nice to me, and so was Steve, who I've kept in touch with. I was very sad when Tony died in March 2014. It was funny that John Golding didn't come over to say hello when I was having dinner with Tony. He's right: if I had seen him I would have made him come over. It's no good Labour MPs not being friends with each other.

MALCOLM

In 1976 I left Keele University. I'd been there since 1964, first as an undergraduate including a year as Students' Union president and then as a research fellow. We moved to Manchester. Three years later Professor W. A. Campbell Stewart retired as vice chancellor of the university, and Neil rang me to tell me who had got the job.

'It's Professor David Harrison from Cambridge, and he's a very nice man.'

'Oh, you know him, then, Neil?'

'Yes, he's a very good friend of mine. When I saw in the Stoke newspaper *The Sentinel* that he's from Cambridge University, I gave him a ring to congratulate him and told him about my connections with Cambridge. He and his wife invited me down to tea, so I went.'

I think Professor Harrison may have been under the impression that Neil was the Anglican chaplain. When he arrived at Keele, I don't know whether he told everyone that his first act as the new VC was to invite Neil Baldwin down to take tea with him. But, actually, if he wanted to learn about Keele, that was as good a starting place as any.

Francis Beckett included that story in an article in *The Guardian* about Neil a quarter of a century later. David Harrison read the article and sent Neil a postcard congratulating him on his fifty years at Keele.

NEIL

Professor Harrison invited me down for a weekend because he wanted to meet me. He'd just had the appointment. I knew he'd been appointed. I managed to find out. And it was in the paper as well. When I saw he was from Cambridge I rang him up. I got through. I said, 'I'm Neil Baldwin from Keele.' He asked me who I was. I said, 'I'm in the church.' He said, 'Come and stay for the weekend.' And we've been friends ever since. The Bishop of Lichfield has the same degree as he had.

In 1979 Mum and I learned that we had to move out of our prefab house in Ripon Avenue because the council had decided to knock it down. At first I was sad, because I had always lived there. I am a Chesterton boy and had a lot of friends there.

But the council rehoused us in a lovely house in the Thistleberry area of Newcastle. It had a garden at the back, and there were no houses opposite, so we could look up at the fields and hill towards Keele. It was a marvellous place to live, because it was nearer to the town centre and easier to get to Stoke City. But what made it really good was that it was much easier to get to Keele because it's just at the bottom of Keele bank, so it's just one short bus ride to get up there.

For many years Mum had been looking after an elderly Christadelphian friend we called Uncle Fred. His wife had died. He lived in Market Drayton, and that meant a forty-mile return trip for Mum several times a week, which made her very tired, but he didn't have anyone else to look after him. All our friends were amazed at how she had the energy and time to drive to Market Drayton to look after Uncle Fred as well as keep on looking after me, giving me lifts, doing my washing, feeding me.

Mum gave Uncle Fred a lot of help and was very upset

when he passed away. He left his house to my mum. That was how she had enough money to eventually buy our house in Thistleberry under the right-to-buy legislation, so she didn't have to pay rent any more. It was very good of him.

CHAPTER FOUR

NELLO THE CIRCUS CLOWN

NEIL

I always loved the circus, particularly the trapeze, ever since my mum had taken me to see it in Stoke. Bailey Fossett was in charge of Fossett's Circus, and he was a very good friend of mine. In the seventies, when I went to the circus, I used to speak to everyone, so they all knew me.

I left Woods, the pottery, in 1980, after fifteen years. That's a long time to work for one firm. I could see that the pottery business was getting worse, and wanted to leave and go into the circus. I said to myself, I would like to be a clown. I've always wanted to be a clown. So I wrote to Sir Robert Fossett's circus and got a job with them as a circus clown, starting in March 1980.

Training for a clown is hard. It's hard work *being* a clown, and, if you don't learn how to do it, you can't get it right. You learn how to fall and get up again. Your clothes have material underneath to break your fall. You learn to throw balls and eggs in the air and catch them, and an egg falls on your face and breaks and all the kids laugh. I had to fall out of a taxi.

They helped me to do it and the second year I went back and they made me principal clown and gave me a £200 bonus. Sometimes I was dressed as a gorilla.

I had to go to Northampton first, then Peterborough. I had never lived away from my mum before. I used to be with the circus from March until November, and then come back home to my mum and Keele. I travelled all over the country with the circus. I loved it, and so did all the children who came to see us.

You can always make people laugh when you get dressed up. That's one thing I learned from being in the circus, which came in useful later on when I became the Stoke City kit man.

The circuses I worked for put me in their caravan at first, but Mum bought me one of my own a few years after. It was a tiny caravan. In the winter we kept it in a garage at the back of Thistleberry Avenue.

Of course, during the winter, when I was not away with the circus, I went to Keele nearly every day, kept the Neil Baldwin Football Club going and was still Rag Safety Officer. You have to keep yourself occupied, don't you?

MALCOLM

One day in 1981, by which time we were living in Sale near Manchester, Neil rang to tell us that Fossett's Circus, in which he was appearing, was visiting Wythenshawe in South

Manchester. We naturally decided to take my two young daughters, Zara and Zoe, to see the show, and arranged to visit him in his caravan beforehand. We found this small, rather dishevelled caravan, with quite amateurish writing on the side. We arrived just as Neil was collecting his tea from the catering van.

He announced that he had a problem, namely that the gorilla suit he was due to wear was badly ripped. Upon examination, it was obviously unwearable.

'Can you stitch it up for me, Lesley?' he asked my wife.

'Of course, Neil. Have you got a needle and thread?' He hadn't, of course, so we visited fellow circus performers to see if one of them could come up with the required equipment. Fortunately, someone did.

Lesley then sat down and undertook extensive repair work to this rather unattractive garment, which, apart from anything else, didn't look as if it had seen the inside of a washing machine for a considerable period. The task was eventually completed and Neil was set up for the show, which we all enjoyed.

'What would have happened if I hadn't been here to repair the suit, Neil?' Lesley asked innocently.

'Somebody would have done it,' Neil replied.

This is probably true. There always is somebody to help Neil out of his scrapes. That's because of who Neil is. People are very willing to help him out, just because he is Neil.

NEIL

It was great to see Malcolm and Lesley and their daughters on that day. The little girls really enjoyed it and I made them laugh. When I went round the country with the circus I always got in touch with anyone I knew in that area, because I knew that they would be disappointed if they had missed the chance to see me.

MALCOLM
He did too. Tony Bartlett recalls: 'Once when he was a clown in Middlesbrough he phoned up my mum and dad. They went to see him in the caravan, did some of his washing and fed him. He is never afraid of asking.'

And Cousin Brenda says:

> When Neil came to Liverpool with the circus he would just ring up out of the blue and ask us to come across the water and pick him up, which wasn't always easy with children, but you do it because it's Neil, and it was always good to see him.

NEIL
In 1981, when the circus was in Cambridge, all the Cambridge Boat Race crew came to see me.

When the circus went to Canterbury I went to see Professor David Ingram and he took me out for a meal. He was the vice chancellor of the University of Kent. Professor Ingram had been a very good friend of mine when he was at Keele. I always thought he would become a vice chancellor somewhere one day. I hoped it might be at Keele. He was a wonderful man who was very involved in the chapel and the Christian groups at Keele. I was sad when he died in 2001.

MALCOLM

David Ingram had been deputy vice chancellor at Keele in the 1960s. He was a charismatic professor of physics, who is remembered by all Keele students because he always gave the very first inspiring lecture on the universe in the unique Keele Foundation Year. He was prominent in the Keele Christian community.

Perry Spillar, who is now one of Radio Stoke's presenters, was a child when he saw Neil for the first time. Perry's father, Dennis, was the vicar in Stratford-upon-Avon, but before that he had been a curate in Clayton, Newcastle-under-Lyme, so of course he knew Neil.

One day Perry heard his father answer the telephone and say, 'Who's this speaking? Oh, it's you, Neil. You're a clown? Really? And you're coming to Stratford upon Avon?'

Dennis then tried to explain to his son who Neil was, but it wasn't easy. Perry says:

> I remember this conversation quite vividly as he tried to tell me why Neil was so well known and popular and exactly how he managed to get so much done. Dad came to the conclusion that Neil was some sort of accidental, natural-born publicity-and-marketing genius. I also remember thinking how strange to go through life with such an unquestioning sense of confidence and expectation, this at a time when I was suffering the usual awkwardness and embarrassment of a teenager, worrying immensely at the smallest of issues. My dad talked to me about Neil's football team.

So I went with my dad to see Neil performing in the circus. There were two clowns, and Neil was the second one. He was dressed as a gorilla. I remember sitting in the circus and we weren't quite certain which one was Neil.

After the show we went to see him in his very small caravan. We were sitting there with washing hanging up all over the caravan while Neil, dressed in the gorilla suit, made us a cup of tea. Quite surreal.

NEIL

I had four summers with Fossett's Circus in England. After that, for the next two summers, I was with circuses in Ireland, first Fossett's in 1984 and Courtenay's in 1985. I wasn't a gorilla any more, just Nello the Clown. We did music and gags. As a clown you register your face colours and make-up pattern and no one else can use them. So it's unique. There's only one Nello. In Ireland we did lots of work with schools, which I really liked. I have always loved entertaining children.

I returned to England with Ray Smith's Galaxy Circus for three years from 1986 to 1988. I also appeared in Hoffman's Circus locally in the Potteries. That was for just one week. That was when I had to fall off the back of a fire engine.

One time I was visiting Cambridge with the circus when Prince Edward was there, and I thought he would like the chance to meet me. I found out where his room was and went to it. I was expecting to find a policeman on the door, but there wasn't one. So I knocked on the door and luckily he was in.

I told him how I love all the royal family and I often write to his mother. He invited me in for a glass of sherry. It was very nice sherry and he is a very nice man, like all the royal family.

MALCOLM
Vic Trigg recalls:

> After leaving Keele, Helen and I kept in close touch with Mary and sometimes saw Neil, who worked in the circus from 1980 to 1989. There were at least a couple of occasions when we collected him from abandoned sites at the end of the circus season. On one occasion it seemed that Neil's disreputable caravan was simply being abandoned at the side of the road once he had vacated it.
>
> Mary got into caravanning herself. I think this was due to her sister Beryl, who had a caravan in the Peak District. Mary bought a caravan of her own in Derbyshire and then moved it to our land at Market Drayton from about 1985 to 1995 and often stayed in it for three to four weeks at a time with her dog, birdwatching, walking and talking to people.

NEIL
At the end of the circus season I asked friends to come and pick me up and bring me home. They didn't mind. Vic and Helen did it once. After my mum had given me my own caravan as a present, that obviously had to be brought home

as well, which was a bit more difficult to do. You need a tow bar to do that.

Nineteen eighty-nine was my last year in the circus. I started with Johnny Fossett's Circus. They were different from Robert Fossett's, although they were related. All the circus families are related to each other, you know, and I know them all. But they had an argument with me. Someone said I wasn't pulling my weight, which was very unfair, and they didn't pay me my proper money, which wasn't fair, either. They gave me the push and just left me on my own in a lay-by somewhere in Leicestershire, which wasn't very nice.

But I went to the local minister and got in touch with Morrison's Circus. They gave me a job and rescued me. They even sent an RAC van and loaded my caravan onto it and took me all the way to Scotland. Morrison's Circus paid for that. That was nice of them, but they must have thought I was a good clown and they wanted me in their circus.

The Morrison's boss had a car accident and the season had to finish early, so I was left stuck in Scotland. To make things worse, my caravan got stolen. I think it was gypsies. I told the police but they didn't do anything. So I went to the local vicar to get some help. I told him who I was and what had happened. It's a good idea to go to a vicar because we Christians will always do what we can to help others. It's what Jesus told us to do in the Bible. I always try to help other people who are in difficulty if I can and I know others will do the same for me.

He got in touch with my mum and they sorted it out. The Scottish vicar gave me a lift halfway back to England. I think it might have been to Dumfries but I might be wrong about that. The English vicar picked me up from there. I think it was the Keele vicar, Mark Turner.

After all that I decided not be a clown anymore and that I would be better looking for a job in football.

There were some important anniversaries around that time, too. Three years earlier, for instance, I'd had my fortieth birthday.

MALCOLM

Cousin Brenda remembers: 'In 1986, Neil placed an advert in *The Times* for his own fortieth birthday, and the bill was invoiced to Auntie Mary. She used to get worried about Neil running up bills for her.'

NEIL

And the year before, 1985, I'd celebrated my twenty-five years at Keele. I asked Dennis Spillar, Perry Spillar's dad, to come up to Keele and take the service of thanksgiving. That was the first of the four services of thanksgiving at Keele that I have had.

MALCOLM

Perry adds:

> When Dad took Neil's service of thanksgiving in 1985, he came up from Stratford-upon-Avon to do so. That's the effect Neil has on people he knows. They are usually willing to do things for him, even if it's quite a lot of trouble.

NEIL

And I didn't forget the NBFC, either. My football team played once against a Coventry team that included Tony Hateley, a great centre-forward who played for a lot of the top clubs.

We lost 14–2. I scored one goal. But it was a good experience for the lads. I told them to learn from it.

I also got a sponsor for my football team. That was the Wheatsheaf pub, which is at Onneley, not far from Keele. We had blue team shirts with 'Wheatsheaf Pub' written on the front, which showed what an important club we were.

We sometimes used to have the annual dinner of NBFC at the Wheatsheaf, and had some good guest speakers. Malcolm was one of them. We sometimes had some Stoke City players there. They thought it was an honour to be invited. I always got presented with the Player of the Year prize at them. Sometimes they did 'This is your life: Neil Baldwin'.

MALCOLM

Stephen Benn remembers those dinners:

> A development of the football club that I remember very clearly was the Neil Baldwin Football Club annual dinner. This was a dress-up occasion, and, though I know I didn't wear a black tie, I'm not entirely sure that Neil didn't. At the dinner I remember in particular he said that there would be a special guest coming to present the prizes, namely Jimmy Greenhoff who played for Stoke City (and would later play for Manchester United).

It was held at the Thistleberry on the Keele Road. Jimmy Greenhoff was a major footballing figure at the time. So for it to be claimed that he would be presenting the prizes sounded very grand. But he was there, and he did just that. There were several different prizes. I think I'm right that Neil was Player of the Year.

NEIL

Yes, he's right. I won Player of the Season every year. And of course I still had an important responsibility as Rag Safety Officer.

MALCOLM

He certainly did, and he took it very seriously. Gary Thomas, a student at that time, recounts how even Rag officials weren't immune from Neil's authority:

Back in 1983, I was Rag Committee secretary, and Neil was our safety officer. That year, the theme of Rag Week was clowns (not because of Neil's background – just coincidental). The culmination of the week involved us going to Newcastle on a low-loader, all dressed as clowns (the costumes made by one of the committee members from sheets and individually customised). Neil didn't disappoint, and arrived dressed as Nello – showing us all how it's done.

We returned on the flatbed, all in high spirits and a little giddy. Approaching the Lodge entrance, I saw two friends walking down the hill. I jumped off the flatbed with my collecting can to accost them, and landed in front of a car, which ground to a halt. I looked up at the cab of the flatbed to see Neil leaning out of the window, looking at me, with his accusative finger pointing at me. I knew I was in trouble.

I caught up with the flatbed and we continued on to Keele. We got off the lorry and Neil got out of the cab and walked towards me. He told me off for being so stupid. 'What would I have told your mum and dad if you'd been run over by that car? Don't ever do that again!' he said. I apologised, knowing he was right. However, it was difficult to take seriously a reprimand delivered by a man dressed as a clown!

NEIL

It's a poor show when you even have to watch what the committee are doing. It's not a very good example, is it? But Gary was a great chap and a very good Rag Secretary. He was a very good friend of mine. I think he learned his lesson.

In 1990 it was time for another celebration because I had been at Keele for thirty years. The service was taken by Chris Kemp, a very good friend of mine, who was a vicar I had met in London at the theological college.

We had two speakers to talk about my life, both of them former presidents of the Students' Union, which was marvellous. One of them was Malcolm and other was Steve Shufflebotham, who had been president in 1977. He calls himself Steve Botham now. He said he dropped the 'Shuffle' so that his kids didn't hate him. That's funny, isn't it? When he was president he was a Liberal, not Labour like most of them, but he was a very good president and a good friend of mine. It was a lovely service.

MALCOLM

Neil, as ever, revelled in the occasion, and it was clear, as it always is, just how much the chapel community at Keele love him. The chapel was full and Neil sang a solo, which he always does at these services.

I had a word with the minister who took the service. He said he had met Neil at theological college in London. He told me that Neil 'seemed to know all the bishops'. That figures!

By then Neil was adjusting to a completely new way of life. The year before, 1989, he had not only left the circus but had moved into his own flat.

His mum Mary was worried about what would happen to Neil when she was no longer around. She wanted to see if he could manage living on his own. She also wanted to teach him some life skills, such as how to shop and do other things that she had done for him. Mary was a far-sighted woman, and she had been thinking and praying about this for some time.

NEIL

My mum suggested that I should move into my own flat. At first I didn't want to because I had always lived with Mum and I was a bit worried about how she would cope without me, but I agreed to it to keep her happy.

I moved into a flat that is only just across the green from where we lived, so it was very easy for me to pop back home every day to help Mum or take Jessie, our dog, out for a walk. It also meant I had more room for all my circus and football programmes and could have more birds to look after, so it worked out well for everyone. Mum also came into my new flat to do some of the cleaning and tidying.

MALCOLM
If he couldn't manage, Mary had a back-up plan. She thought he might go to live at Cerne Abbas Monastery in Dorset, where Neil went to stay for a couple of weeks. He was accepted to go to live there after Mary died.

NEIL
I enjoyed staying at the monastery at Cerne Abbas for two weeks because it's a very pretty village and of course a very holy place. I helped the monks making honey.

I know that Mum meant well when she thought of it and fixed it up. She said that I should only go to live there if I wanted to, but I didn't because it's far too far from Keele University and Stoke City, and there aren't any football pitches for the Neil Baldwin Football Club to play on.

So I still live in the same flat. It's very good because it's easy to get to Keele or into town on the bus.

MALCOLM
James Townend, a Keele student, remembers his first meeting with Neil in the early 1990s and then playing for NBFC:

I have very happy memories of playing a few

matches for NBFC and of Neil himself. He certainly left his mark on myself and friends at the time.

I have vivid memories of my first encounter with Neil on my first night at university. Neil was sat in the reception of the Students' Union, in the place he was always to be found for the next four years, trying to sign people up for his football team, which a keen few of us, not really knowing what to make of this larger-than-life character, did.

We were a bit sceptical of his claims about people whom he knew and things he had done, but it soon became apparent that they were true. We soon got to hear the stories of him applying for the England job, being Stoke kit man, and our doubts were cast aside when one day, not long afterwards at the sports hall, we saw him sat having a pizza with [the then Stoke manager] Lou Macari.

A couple of matches stand out – one a day out to Cambridge, which was just brilliant from the journey down in an old minibus, listening to Neil's stories for the whole journey, to the tour round the grounds of the university, to the match on the pristine pitch. I can't remember the result but I seem to feel like we won. I'm sure Neil has detailed records of each match.

The other was the match Neil organised for us to play at Newcastle Town's ground against a guest eleven – it was for some sort of anniversary but I can't remember what exactly – and Neil had managed to get the Liverpool legend David Fairclough to play in the game. I do seem to remember that I kicked him in the first couple of minutes, and he wasn't too happy about that. I recall Neil coming onto the pitch for the last five or ten minutes.

I also remember his fairly frequent visits to our block in Horwood Hall at Keele on the pretence of talking football, but I suspect he was more there for the tea and biscuits. I have a memory of his staying in my room for beans on toast at one point.

NEIL

It was a great game to raise money for charity at Newcastle Town. We played a team of old stars. We won 5–0. I wrote to David Fairclough at Liverpool to get him to come, and then rang him up. He only played the first half because he didn't like getting kicked. Gordon Banks played, but not in goal.

CHAPTER FIVE

THE STOKE CITY KIT MAN

NEIL

I applied for the job as Stoke City manager but they didn't give it to me. They gave it to Lou Macari in the summer of 1991, and I got to know Lou very soon after he got the job. I knew he would want to meet me as soon as possible. All the managers do. Lou's a very nice man and a very good friend of mine.

MALCOLM

Lou Macari was appointed as Stoke's manager in the summer of 1991. Neil, of course, was still a regular outside the ground and the training ground and he soon came to know Lou.

In his autobiography, *Football, My Life*, Lou recalls meeting Neil at a 'Meet the Manager' evening, when Neil wished him all the best. 'Thanks very much,' said Lou. 'What do you do?'

'I'm a circus clown.'

'Oh, really? And what do you do in your act?'

'They throw me off the back of a fire engine.'

'What, every night?'

'Yes.'

As we have seen, Neil had in fact ended his career as a circus clown in 1989. Lou describes in his autobiography the decision to appoint him kit man:

> I detected a character in my midst. I decided he was the man for me and Nello eventually became the kit man. That was a promotion. Before that his role was to make me laugh and the players.
>
> Nello had a heart of gold; the club did not pay him a penny. He did it all for love and we loved having him around. His real value was in helping the players relax before games. No chemist ever produced a drug that could reduce stress levels like Nello. I was convinced that this gave us an edge in matches. Nello bonded the group.

He describes Neil as his 'best ever signing in football'.

NEIL

Lou offered me the job as kit man after he had been at Stoke for a few weeks. I was really pleased because I had been a Stoke fan all my life and knew I could help him and the team.

At first my mum didn't believe that I was going to be kit man. She didn't think I could look after the kit and do washing, because she had done all that for me. Stoke City didn't pay me, but I didn't mind. I did it for love. Lou says I am his best ever signing, and he's right. My mum used to speak to Lou and she loved him because of what he did for me. She knew he would look after me.

MALCOLM

At first *I* didn't really believe it, either. Neither did most of Neil's friends. But we should have known better.

Ivan Gaskell, who was Radio Stoke's Stoke City reporter at the time, remembers Lou and then Neil arriving at the club.

> Lou was energetic and charismatic. Almost immediately there was a different atmosphere in the ground. It was more relaxed. One day I turned up to interview Lou and in the corner of his office was Nello, who Lou introduced as his personal assistant. He just sat there with a grin on his face. He had simply appeared from nowhere and I knew nothing about him; no explanation was given on who he was.
>
> I visited the club at least two or three times a week. Nello just immersed himself in the fabric of the dressing room. At first I couldn't work out who he was or why he was there. I think it was a deliberate tactic by Lou, and Nello had a specific role. Lou wanted to introduce fun, humour and

lightness around the place. Neil was just there, a sort of stooge, someone to bounce off, a random element. Something different.

I spent many hours in the corridor waiting for interviews. There was often constant laughter, with Nello moving from one room to the next; there was shouting and banter. It was often directed at Neil, but he also gave it back. He would be in the sauna in fancy dress; the whole thing was slightly bizarre and surreal. It made my work far more interesting and definitely unforgettable.

But Neil was very smart, with a sparkle in his eye. In his own way he was quite a smart cookie. He was living his dream, but also he brought something to the table. He was quite canny.

Players used to let off steam directed at Neil, and some of the banter had an edge to it. But I think over time Nello melted that away and they came to love him.

To some extent I think Lou was trying to wind the players up. I suspect some of them railed against it at first because the dressing room tends to be the players' inner sanctum and some of them thought it not very professional to have somebody like Nello in the dressing room. But Lou brought in strong characters and ultimately good guys and they accepted Neil in the end.

Adrian Hurst, who worked for the club (and is still employed at the club, at the time of writing, as community manager) says, 'I'm sure Lou saw it as a form of stress relief.'

At the time I assumed he was employed and getting paid in the normal way. I was very surprised when I finally found out that he wasn't. So, after he left, I asked the club to give him a free season ticket for life, in return for his not being paid for all those years, which they readily agreed to do.

The decision to take Neil on in what was effectively a full-time job without paying him a wage could be regarded as risky in employment and insurance terms (particularly if anything had happened to Neil, for example, as he wheeled the large heavy skips of kit from the coach to the dressing rooms at away games). But Neil has never seen anything wrong with the arrangement. He was just delighted to be involved with the club he loves.

Neil wasn't really in charge of the kit. That task fell to the longstanding kit manager Winnie Hudson, who was employed by Stoke throughout Neil's time there. She was responsible for ensuring that the kit was properly washed and that the first team's kit was available and in good order on match days.

The only thing that Winnie did not always do, which Neil did, was to accompany the team to away matches. She was a key figure in Neil's time at Stoke City because, after he joined the club, Winnie had another important role: that of showing Neil the ropes and helping him, looking out for him and, on occasions, making sure that any teasing, practical jokes or even bullying directed at Neil by the players or other staff did not go too far.

NEIL

Winnie was great. She was the best kit manager in the country. She was behind the scenes but she gave great service to Stoke City. She always looked after me and was a bit like a mum to me. I helped her look after the kit and get it ready.

We were a very good team, a better team than the players sometimes, as I used to tell them. I really enjoyed being the kit man helping her. Sometimes if she wasn't there I would do some of the washing. She couldn't always go into the dressing room if the players were getting changed, so I did that. There was always banter in there. I had my own black 'Carling' sponsor's tracksuit with my initials 'NB' on it, just like the players and the manager, because the kit man is very important.

MALCOLM

Adrian Hurst remembers the roles of both Winnie and Neil:

> Winnie was a mother figure to Neil. That was evident from Day One. I remember meeting Neil for the first time. He was a larger-than-life character, but at first I didn't appreciate his vulnerability.
>
> Neil was very proud of what he was doing, and wanted to do it well – for example, when he was cleaning boots. He used to spend ages carefully cutting up strips of Lycra for the players' socks.
>
> He really enjoyed being there. Everyone else enjoyed him being there. It created an atmosphere of infectious good fun.
>
> The players were very good to him on a one-

to-one basis, but sometimes there was a gang mentality when they were together with a lot of fun at Neil's expense. This occasionally went too far, such as when he was locked in the sauna, which was intended as a bit of fun but was not sensible. Neil normally took it all in his stride, and he always walked off with a throwaway line back at them, but very occasionally he could get a bit upset and aggressive in response.

He had a great relationship with the teenage apprentice player lads, even though they used to throw trainers at him, very hard. I didn't always like the things which happened, but, if Lou was around, it would be dealt with. Nello stayed for years, so he must have been happy.

Some others who were at the club at that time have told me that sometimes they felt uncomfortable about the things that were done to Neil, such as removing his clothes on a coach journey, but that it was really down to Lou to decide if things had gone too far. If he didn't do anything about it, it didn't really fall to anyone else to do so. But Neil himself takes a very positive view.

NEIL

All the players liked me. Some of them were really kind to me. There was only one who was very nasty, and I think Lou might have got rid of him partly because of the way he treated me. But I'm not going to say who it was because what does it matter now? It's all in the past. The practical jokes were just a bit of fun. There's always jokes and banter with football players. You just have to accept it, and give them some back. I remember being locked in the sauna, but they were only having a laugh. They didn't succeed in getting my clothes off on the bus. Sometimes I got my own back. I was very happy, and was Lou's right-hand man. He's still a very good friend of mine.

MALCOLM

One of the players, Lee Sandford, saw Neil's contribution like this:

> When Lou Macari got the job he gave Neil the job as kit man and it was clever because it took the pressure off the players. He became part of the furniture. It worked, the team was successful, and Neil was a hundred per cent part of that success and contributed to it in his own way.
>
> He was the butt of jokes, but he gave it out as well. When we were going to away games, Neil was such a massive character that everything reflected onto him and not the players because of the humour and the banter, and Lou was clever enough to use that. It worked really well.
>
> We had big silver laundry skips that the kit went into, and they were so big that if we put Neil into one of them he couldn't get out. At the Victoria Ground the tunnel's on a slope and we put him in one of the skips and rolled it down the tunnel. He'd laugh it off.

But sometimes Winnie would come and tell us off and then we'd stop. Winnie was a lovely lady and she was also part of the success of the team. She was great. She looked after us childish footballers. She did the hard work; Neil was the fun and games.

Martin Carruthers, another player, about whom we shall hear more later, also recalls Neil's and Winnie's roles:

We had banter with Nello every day. Sometimes we'd throw him in a cold bath or wheel him round the pitch in the shopping trolley they used for the dirty kit. If it went a bit too far for him he'd go shouting for Winnie, the kit woman. Winnie and Nello washed all the players' kit, and they brought it back in a shopping trolley. It was Nello's job to bring it back in the shopping trolley, and often he'd end up *in* the trolley, and he'd be screaming for Winnie. Winnie was his guardian angel. Whenever he was in trouble with the lads or we were trying to get him to do something he didn't want to do, Winnie would come along, and the lads would listen to Winnie. Sometimes she thought it was funny, but sometimes she would bawl us out and then we'd stop. Winnie was brilliant. She had a lot of banter with Nello as well.

The first time I spoke to Neil was after I signed for Stoke, and there was a clause in my contract that said they were going to give me a holiday. So

I went to see Lou Macari about it and Nello was in Lou's office and Lou said, 'Nello, take this lad to the travel agent and book him a holiday.' I thought, This is a joke. But Nello took me to the travel agent – they all knew him there, he was famous around Stoke, more famous than the players – and he said, 'Where do you want to go?' And Nello and the travel agent showed me a few brochures and I said, 'Ibiza.' so Nello booked me a holiday in Ibiza.

Then he took me back to Lou Macari's office. Everyone else knocked when they went to Lou Macari's office but Nello just walked in.

One time, I hadn't been in the team for a couple of weeks, so one afternoon after training I went and knocked on Lou Macari's office door to ask him why I hadn't been in the team. Nello was sitting there with some coffee, and I said, 'I'm doing well. I think I deserve to be in the team.' Lou Macari said, 'Tell him, Nello.' And Nello said, 'It's because you're no good, Carruthers, now go away.' I didn't know what to say, so I just walked out.

Ivan Gaskell says:

I think at times it trod a very fine line between what was acceptable and what went too far, and occasionally I asked myself whether something was right and whether Neil was accepting it because he didn't want to lose the role he had. It was a different era, and much of those things just wouldn't happen now. But I trusted Lou, who's a good guy, to make sure that the line wasn't crossed.

Nello also wanted to be taken as an equal. Banter and practical jokes are very much part of the dressing room. But I also knew that Nello could look after himself and stand up for himself. I only saw him thrive. His role evolved and he was given the title of kit man, which he took extremely seriously. I can remember him saying proudly to me, 'I'm the kit man now, you know.'

One Stoke City fan on the 'Oatcake' Internet message board (*Oatcake* is the name of the club's fanzine) remembers that Neil was quite clear how important his role was:

When I was a kid, I was getting autographs of the players in my autograph book after training when this bloke came up to me, snatched the book, signed it and passed it back to me. I later found out it was the kit man, Baldwin.

NEIL

Lots of people ask me for my autograph now. Maybe an early example would be worth something.

Ivan Gaskell is a very good friend of mine. He is a very good football reporter. I told him recently that I'm now more famous than he is. I did all the different jobs that Lou asked me to do. Sometimes you have to hold players' hands with things like holidays, so I didn't mind going to the travel agent with Martin to help him.

One day Lou suddenly wanted me to lose weight and tried to control my diet. I think my mum had suggested it to him. I wasn't too keen on that, but I know she meant well.

MALCOLM

Jesse 'Twinny' Doyle, a Stoke fan who used to work on Stoke market in those days, remembers: 'Neil used to come across to the market to buy his lunch. I remember him going to the fruit stall, and saying with a long face that Lou had put him on a diet and he had to buy fruit.'

Adrian Hurst recalls:

He told me he was a clown, but I didn't really believe him. Once, the circus set up on the Victoria Ground car park. Nello said we would go down, as he knew them all. As we walked through the caravans it became rapidly apparent that he was very well known to the circus community; all the circus acts knew him as he knocked on their caravan doors. They told me he was a very good friend and greeted him, '*Neil!* How *are* you?' We got cups of tea made for us. I got two complimentary tickets and we were treated like royalty. From that day on I always knew Neil's claims to be well known in the circus community were true.

NEIL

Of course they were true. I'm well known in the circus because I was a very good clown. I think Adrian believes me now if I say I know someone.

We always played five-a-side against the young lads, the apprentice players, on a Friday. Lou and Chic Bates used to play. We usually beat them easy. I was a good keeper and the young lads didn't like losing to us. I also took some good penalties, and I still take good penalties.

MALCOLM
Adrian recalls:

> I remember five-a-side football matches between the staff and second-year apprentice players. Neil went in goal for the staff wearing purple mittens, which he struggled to get on. Agility wasn't his strong point, but of course he filled the goal. The staff often won the game. The young lads were a bit lippy with him, but he simply responded, 'You didn't score any goals and you didn't win.'
>
> On Nello's fiftieth birthday [in 1996] someone organised a stripper of rather large proportions in the Blue Room at the Victoria Ground. Others might have been embarrassed but Neil just took it all in his stride.

NEIL
I don't know why they thought it funny to send that strange woman. I don't like that kind of stuff, so I told them all off. They liked to play their little games. I suppose you have to let them have their kind of fun. But a lot of players came to my proper fiftieth-birthday party up at Keele, which was marvellous. That was a great night.

MALCOLM

Neil's first season as kit man, and Lou's as manager, 1991/92, had been very successful. It included a 2–2 draw against Liverpool at Anfield in the Rumbelows Cup (as the League Cup was then called), which was memorable for us for two reasons. First, my youngest daughter Lisa was the Stoke mascot that night. Second, Stoke's equaliser, late in the game, was scored by Tony Kelly, who, as we shall see, was later to play a significant part in Neil's story. Although Stoke were denied promotion by being knocked out in the play-offs by Stockport County, they gained revenge a few days later by beating them at Wembley in the final of the League Trophy (then called the Autoglass Trophy).

Ivan Gaskell recalls:

I remember the Autoglass Final against Stockport County. As was common, the squad went down to stay in a hotel not too far from Wembley a few days before the final. I accompanied the squad.

Nello was there. I remember karaoke at the local pub with full renditions from all sorts of people – including Nello, who showed he could sing – Chick Bates, the assistant manager, Tony Lacy, the coach, and Ian Bailey from *The Sentinel*.

There was an afternoon training session of five-a-side with the team on the day before the Cup Final, and amazingly, all of us played, including Nello. This is the day before a Cup Final, would you believe, and we are playing with the team. I think Lou wanted to reduce the tension and it worked.

NEIL

We won the Autoglass Trophy because I had shown them how to do it the day before in that practice game.

We used to have pre-season tours abroad. In my first couple of years at Stoke. These were to the Isle of Man, where they had a good football tournament with other clubs. We won it both times in 1991, beating Sunderland in the final, and 1992, when we thrashed Wrexham in the final. I told the team that was great, and that, if they played like that in the League, we would win it, which we did. We won the League Two Championship with ninety-three points, including a club record run of twenty-five undefeated games. Mark Stein became the first player to score thirty goals in a season for thirty years.

MALCOLM

Andrew Edwards, who was later to organise the funerals of Mary Gandey and Sir Stanley Matthews, recalls one of those tournaments in the Isle of Man. Andrew is a prominent local funeral director and a friend of Stoke City's vice chairman, Keith Humphries. Andrew and Keith stayed in the Castletown Golf Links Hotel and took in some golf.

While they were on the golf links, they ran into some Stoke City players. Apparently one of the players, Steve Foley, was a very keen ornithologist, unlikely though that will seem to many Stoke supporters who have watched his style of play; and Steve was leading them on the walk. Neil was with them.

Andrew recalls:

Keith Humphries and I were on the first tee when they returned and surrounded us to watch. Neither of us were very good golfers. I promptly managed to put the first three balls into the gorse, to the great amusement of the watching company.

Nello went into Douglas [the Isle of Man capital] with some others to do some shopping. They came back with a child's golf set made of plastic. Nello formally presented it to me in the hotel foyer in recognition of the golfing prowess which they had witnessed on that first tee. I was asked to demonstrate my golfing skills. The toy ball was placed on a glass table, and I swung the plastic golf club to hit it. Unfortunately, my swing hit the table, which promptly shattered into a thousand pieces.

Nello, of course, found this highly amusing and for some time mercilessly retold the story of how 'Mr Edwards is so useless at golf that he even broke a hotel glass table with a child's plastic golf club' to anyone who would listen.

But he was great fun to have on those trips and added light-hearted amusement to the group. He's a character, there's no doubt about that, and a true Stokie.

NEIL

I didn't imagine Mr Edwards would be a football hooligan. I think he could have improved his golf with practice. We won the Isle of Man tournament both years when I was there, which is not surprising.

I think I also helped win the league in 1992–3. Apart from telling the players that they needed to keep scoring goals and not let any in, that was when I started sitting on the bench in a variety of fancy dresses. The first of these was an away game at Hartlepool just before Christmas 1992.

MALCOLM

I can still remember our disbelief as Neil followed the team out of the dressing room wearing a top hat and tails. We had never seen anything like that at a football match before.

Lou Macari gave the background to this in his autobiography. The team were staying overnight in a posh hotel and Lou arranged for Neil to travel in a dinner suit and bow tie and top hat, which he wore for dinner in the restaurant. Lou introduced him to the waiters as 'Lord Baldwin from Keele'. The waiters gave him special attention and at the end of the meal offered him a box of cigars with the words, 'Would you like to choose a cigar, Lord Baldwin?' Neil apparently was in his element, proudly enjoying his cigar. Everyone else was in hysterics.

Next day when he came down to breakfast in his normal tracksuit, Lou told him to go and get changed and wear the full dinner suit. So he became the first kit man to carry the bag wearing a top hat, and probably the last. The players found it hilarious, which was no doubt Lou's intention.

NEIL

All the people in that hotel thought I really was Lord Baldwin of Keele, but that's actually a good name, isn't it? I think that, when I am made a lord, I will call myself 'Lord Baldwin of Keele'. I've also been called the Bishop of Keele. I'm not sure which is better. The top hat only just fitted into the dugout. But it helped us win the game 2–1. Nigel Gleghorn scored right at the end. I wonder if my DJ put the Hartlepool players off.

A couple of months later at an away game at Leyton Orient I came out as a Mutant Ninja Turtle. But this time something went wrong: a defeat on a snowy day saw the end of the wonderful twenty-five-game unbeaten run.

Just a couple of weeks later Lou was at it again, this time getting me to dress up in a bright-yellow chicken suit for an away game at Bournemouth. Lou and I bought the chicken suit together. All the way down to the game on the team coach, I kept the suit on, including the chicken's head. Malcolm and his daughter Zara were standing just behind the dugout, and they couldn't believe it when I came out dressed as a yellow chicken.

The game was a draw. Nigel Gleghorn had to go in goal when Ronnie Sinclair had to leave the field injured, and had a great game. Nigel was a very good goalkeeper, even though he was a midfield player.

The chicken suit was really hot, and I was sweating very heavily, but Lou wouldn't let me take it off all day. In the end I did. It was marvellous to see the crowd laughing at a yellow chicken appearing on the touchline. One of the things I learned in the circus is that getting dressed up always makes people laugh. But it is more difficult to carry the big kit bag when you are dressed as a chicken.

MALCOLM

We went to the game with a Stoke-supporting friend who had moved to Yeovil. I can still remember his jaw dropping when he saw the yellow chicken come out. You just don't expect things like that to happen on a professional football field.

It helped relax the players – though they weren't always sure they approved, as Lee Sandford told me:

> Sometimes it rubbed us up the wrong way. You want to be professional and it's hard when there's a bloke there dressed as a clown or a duck. And sometimes, when we lost, Neil would shout out something we didn't appreciate on the coach back. But Lou encouraged him and I think it was Lou's way of saying things to us.

The season ended with one of the most memorable matches in my fifty-plus years of watching Stoke City, although on paper you wouldn't expect this game to be at all memorable, and for most of the game it wasn't. Here's what happened.

Gordon Cowans had been a stalwart for Aston Villa. Stoke City were invited to play Aston Villa in his testimonial on 11 May 1993. The attendance was only 4,500, of whom nearly half were travelling Stoke City supporters.

After about an hour, Mark Stein, Stoke's star centre-forward, was taken off. He peeled off his No. 9 shirt and was seen to hand it to Neil, who was struggling to put it on – a bit of a squeeze given Neil's size. Towards the end of the game, we saw Neil lumbering up and down the touchline doing a sort of warm-up.

'Look at Neil,' said Zara. 'What's he doing?'

'Well, it looks as though he is trying to warm up,' I said.

'Why's he doing that?'

'I don't know, it's very odd.'

George Andrews was a Radio Stoke reporter covering the game. His boss, George Gavin, was there too, and as Neil warmed up he said:

'Who on earth is that?'

'It's the kit man and mascot. I think Lou is going to bring him on.'

'Never!!'

But as Neil's warm-up continued, a buzz started to develop among the supporters. Some started singing, 'Bring him on!' And about five minutes from the end of the game, Neil entered the field of play. In fact, Stoke didn't take a player off, so, for the last few minutes, Stoke had twelve players on the field. The referee was Kieron Richardson who refereed the Cup Final that season. This could be a good quiz question: 'When did the Cup Final referee allow a team to play with twelve men on the pitch?'

Neil immediately began pointing and shouting instructions to the other players. He wasn't in the least fazed or nervous.

In his autobiography, Lou recalls how he called over Vince Overton, the Stoke City captain, and told him to tell the Stoke players and the Villa players to let Neil score. It seems that everybody on the pitch understood what was going on, including Nigel Spink, the Villa goalkeeper, except one player: Stoke City's Tony Kelly.

The Aston Villa side included Martin Carruthers, later a Stoke player, who recalls the match:

> The first time I saw Nello, I was still at Aston Villa. I was on the pitch for the testimonial game against Stoke and the Stoke management team had a word with our management team, they said they are going to put their kit man on the pitch, let him through to score a goal.
>
> It had all been agreed for Nello to score. All the Aston Villa players were going to let Nello through to score, but then a Stoke player, Tony Kelly, bundled Nello out of the way and took the shot himself, and missed. He wanted the glory himself. It was a shame. It would have been Nello's dream. If Tony Kelly hadn't taken the ball away from him, he'd have got a shot and the goalkeeper would have stayed out of the way.

NEIL

Martin Carruthers played well that day and scored one of the goals for Aston Villa, who beat us 4–1. That was probably why Lou signed him up for Stoke City.

It was marvellous to make my debut for Stoke City. I was really pleased when Lou told me he was going to put me on. It had always been a dream to play for Stoke City. If he had put me on earlier, we might have pulled the game round.

I was about to score, but Tony Kelly took the ball off me and missed. If he had left it to me I would definitely have scored. He denied me the chance to score for Stoke City and I have never forgotten that.

At the end of the game, England international David Platt, who was playing for Villa, asked me to swap shirts. I bet my shirt is one of his prize possessions.

MALCOLM

At the end of the official club video of that season, Ivan Gaskell did an interview with Lou Macari in which he talks of the signing of a mystery Scottish striker. The overweight 'striker' (Neil), dressed in a kilt and sporran, then wanders into shot behind Macari, and lifts his kilt to reveal a very large stomach, while Macari talks in a deadpan voice of his 'doing his talking on the pitch' but 'not being in the best of condition'. Eventually, he and Ivan can contain themselves no longer and dissolve into hysterical laughter. It still receives multiple hits on YouTube to this day (If you're interested, the link is: https://www.youtube.com/watch?v=O2h6qyEIVGw.)

Ivan recalls:

> For the Scottish-striker film, which was at the end of the season, I can't remember whose idea it was but I do know that Lou definitely wanted Nello involved. Lou played the part brilliantly. I could see Nello dressed up off screen. He was in my eye line, but not Lou's. Lou's straight face was hilarious. After it was over we laughed continuously for about three or four minutes.

NEIL

It was very funny making that film. I loved getting dressed up in the Scottish clothes. Everybody loves looking at it. You can see that I was a film star making people laugh even then, and I still am. You can always make people laugh when you dress up in fancy dress. I learned that in the circus.

MALCOLM

Ivan says:

> Both Lou and Neil have hearts of gold. When I left the area to pursue my career elsewhere, I was very touched when Lou turned up with Nello at my leaving do. In the end it was Nello holding court and I almost slipped away unnoticed. But both Nello and Lou said good things about me, which meant a great deal to me.

NEIL

Before the 1993–4 season I went with the team to Tanzania, which seemed a very funny place to go for a pre-season tour. I had never been to Africa before. We went out to the pictures in Dar es Salaam and it wasn't like going to the pictures at home. The cinema was a very poor building and so were all the houses. The cinema was not much more than a mud hut, and Lou and I were the only people in it. Everybody who lived there was very poor and it upset me. I didn't like it at all. It is important to support things like the charity Comic Relief, which helps people in the poor parts of the world. But at least we did win all the four games, scoring twelve goals.

MALCOLM

Lou Macari remembers that trip to the cinema. 'We went in an antiquated vehicle which passed for a taxi in that country and we had no idea where we were. On the journey back, I said to Neil "What would you do if this taxi broke down now in the middle of nowhere?" He just said: "Ring for another one."'

Tony Kelly, who had denied Neil his goal in the testimonial, was the inspiration for another Neil incident at that time. Martin Smith and Dave Frith, the editors of the *Oatcake*, the Stoke City fanzine, told me:

> For the first issue of the 1993–4 season we ran a spoof tabloid story in the back page of the *Oatcake*. It was a Nello 'play me or sell me' ultimatum to the manager, Lou Macari. It was a spoof of an actual demand made by Tony Kelly the season before, who quite clearly had become frustrated by only occasional substitute appearances.

The *Oatcake* headline was 'City kit man holds out for better deal'. The story ran:

> Stoke City kit man Neil 'Nello' Baldwin delivered a crushing blow to the club just hours before the start of the new season by refusing to sign a new contract.
>
> It was the last thing the Potters needed as they prepared to commence their first season back in the First Division since 1990. Nello has become an

intricate part of the set-up at the Victoria ground and there are growing suggestions that he is the brains behind Lou Macari's dynamic managerial style, a rumour that Macari was quickly to denounce as 'garbage'.

Following his appearance for the Stoke City's team friendly at Weston-super-Mare and Villa Park, Nello has had his appetite for first team football whetted and as he was quick to point out, 'I think I have something to offer the team, besides which I don't think I played any worse than any of the other players in our 1–4 defeat at Villa so I'm giving Lou a "play me or sell me" ultimatum.'

Nello is also known to be dissatisfied with his salary, which he believes does not reflect the multitude of tasks he is expected to carry out at the club. Tasks which include not only looking after the kit, but also bearing the brunt of all the players' jokes, cutting Johnny Butler's hair, and dressing up in a variety of fancy dress costumes. Said Nello, 'Vince Overson wouldn't dress up as a Teenage Mutant Ninja Turtle for the kind of money I'm getting so I don't see why I have to.'

Lou is desperate to hang on to a man he sees as being vital to the future success of Stoke City and reportedly offered Nello a contract that would make him the highest paid kit manager in the history of the club. Lou added, 'If we are serious about challenging for the Premier League then

Nello is an important part of our plans, we've already hired a Madonna outfit, with the pointy tits, for when we play at Old Trafford, besides he makes a damned good cup of coffee.'

If City are unable to reach an amicable agreement with their star kit man then there are already a number of clubs lurking in the shadows ready to pounce. Leading the way are Potteries no hopers Port Vale whose manager Johnny Rudge is quoted as saying, 'Who'd have thought that ten years ago we would be in a position to swoop for Stoke City's kit manager? It's a magnificent achievement and sign of the progress we have made over the last ten years.'

Smith and Frith recall:

Lou saw that article and jumped completely on board with the spoof. He organised a leaving do for Nello, complete with farewell banners and a finger buffet of sandwiches and sausage rolls et cetera, claiming he couldn't offer him first-team football and he had to let him go to Port Vale.

Neil eventually managed to convince Lou that our story wasn't true, prompting the City boss to ring us up, on behalf of the legal firm of 'Sue, Grab It and Run', demanding a written apology and '£10,000 in damages'. I can tell you that it's quite something when the Stoke manager rings you up out of the blue like that! We went along with it, typed up an apology and delivered it to the ground with an Italian ten-thousand-lira note (worth about £5 at the time). Lou had the letter and the money pinned to the notice board at the club, although we heard that Nello had been very keen to get his hands on the money.

Things were wrapped up beautifully a few days later when I saw Neil down near the ground and he pulled me over. He very gently said that although he knew the play-me-or-sell-me story had been a joke, could I please be careful about running any more like that in the future because Lou thought we were being serious? It was a wonderful little episode, which captured perfectly the atmosphere at the club back then and showed the sheer spirit at the Victoria Ground. We've moved on to bigger and better things these days, but there is part of us that yearns for the way things were back then as well, and the Stoke City manager could do something like employing Nello and taking the time to enjoy little capers like this one.

At the end of October 1993, Lou Macari suddenly left the club. He had always said that there were only two clubs he would ever leave Stoke City for: Manchester United and Glasgow Celtic. Unfortunately for Stoke City, it was Celtic who came calling.

NEIL

I was sad when Lou went. He offered me the chance to go with him to Celtic, but how could I leave Stoke, my mum and Keele? Joe Jordan took over, having moved from Heart of Midlothian (or Hearts). Joe was also very good to me, but he was a bit more miserable than Lou. He had strict rules. He kept weighing me to watch my weight. I didn't like that, but my mum did.

MALCOLM

However, there were some bright spots around that time. Ivan Gaskell recalls a trip to Italy for Joe Jordan's second game in charge:

> I remember playing away at Padova [Padua] in the Anglo-Italian Cup in November 1993. A group of us, including myself, Nello and George Andrews, were in a gondolier on a day trip to Venice. We were singing very loudly. We had a huge amount of fun and couldn't take anything too seriously.

NEIL

Ivan is right. I'm a very good singer. That was a marvellous day in Venice. We sang the 'Just One Cornetto' song – the one from the Cornetto adverts – along all those canals. I enjoyed some Cornettos as well. But we lost the game 3–0, so I think some of the players might have been having a few Cornettos. I told them that you can't expect to win cups if you let in goals like that and don't score any.

MALCOLM

Stoke City were playing away to Grimsby Town at their Blundell Park ground on 15 January 1994. It was a dreadful goal-less draw. Neil spotted my daughter Zara and me in the crowd and came over for a word.

'Are you at home next Friday evening?'

'Yes,' I said. 'Why?'

'Because I'm coming up to Manchester to see Ken Dodd, who's on at the Palace Theatre. Can I stay with you?'

'Of course. How are you getting up to Manchester?'

'I'll get Asa to give me a lift to the theatre.' Asa Hartford was the assistant manager and lived in the Northwest. 'And will you come to pick me up from the theatre after the show?' As ever, that was more of an instruction than a question.

NEIL

Ken Dodd has been a very good friend of mine for years. I always go to see his shows when he plays in Hanley. I take presents for him and his partner Anne.

MALCOLM

The veteran Liverpudlian comedian Ken Dodd, who became eighty-seven in November 2014 and is still performing regularly at the time of writing, told me:

> Over the years I've had lots and lots of supporters. I don't like the word 'fans' because it sounds too much like fanatic. These are supporters who have become friends, stage-door Johnnies and stage-

door Jennies. Neil's been one of the very best of them for many years. It's a great privilege to be an entertainer and a great privilege to receive the praise that supporters like Neil give you.

Neil's always been there when we played in the Potteries, always smiling, always having something nice to say. He always brings presents like chocolates for us. At first I thought he was an ordinary stage-door Johnny, but I realised that he has a remarkable personality. He's a very kind man. Friendship is obviously very important to him. You think he's not altogether with it, but there's a driving force behind what he does. He's brave, courageous, a one-off. He's a remarkable young man.

You don't *make* people laugh. Laughter's inside them. You have to wrinkle it out, but I didn't ever need to do that with Neil. His beaming face makes you feel good.

So I shouldn't have been surprised at where I found Neil that night in Manchester. It was late in the evening when I turned up at the theatre to fulfil my mission, but could not see any sign of Neil, even though the show had ended some time before. Eventually, one of the staff clearing up suggested that the only place he could possibly be was with Ken Dodd in his dressing room. And so it proved. It was after midnight before we finally set off on the journey back to Sale, where I live.

NEIL

The day before the Ken Dodd show, the former Manchester United manager Sir Matt Busby died, so I said to Malcolm on the way home, 'Do we go anywhere near Old Trafford?' Malcolm said we drove right past it, so I asked him to stop there so I could pay my respects.

There was a sea of memorial flowers for Sir Matt outside Old Trafford, which is Manchester United's stadium. But I wanted to be there because Sir Matt was very good to me. Malcolm didn't realise I knew Sir Matt, but he ought to have known, really.

So we paid our respects, then Malcolm started driving to his home in Sale, and I knew that Nigel Gleghorn, who had gone in goal in the 'chicken' game at Bournemouth, lived in Sale. So I asked if we went anywhere near his house, and Malcolm said no, which showed he knew where Nigel's house was. So I said, 'Can we? I want to make sure he's in bed on the night before a match.' Stoke were playing at home to Oxford United the following day. So, a detour took us past Nigel's house, which was in darkness, and that was all right.

You have to make sure these players do as they should do, and go to bed early before a game.

MALCOLM

The following morning there was a ring on the doorbell. I answered it to find a man I did not recognise on the doorstep.

'Is Nello ready?'

'Ready for what? Who are you?'

The guy announced himself as one of Stoke City's scouts

in Greater Manchester. He explained that he had agreed to pick Neil up from our house before taking him to watch a schoolboy game he was attending, following which he would give Neil a lift down to the Victoria Ground. Neil had not mentioned anything about this to me, so no alarms had been set.

'I'm afraid he's not up yet and he hasn't had his breakfast, which he definitely won't want to miss.'

My visitor was clearly rather irritated to hear this news, and explained he had driven a long way out of his way round the motorway from near Oldham to pick Neil up. He said that he hadn't got time to wait for Neil to get ready, because he would miss some of the schoolboy game he was due to watch. He went on his way with a resigned shake of the head.

When Neil eventually emerged from his room and I related this to him, he was very apologetic that he had forgotten to mention it the night before.

'But how am I going to get down to the Victoria Ground in time to meet Joe's deadline? I'll be in trouble if I'm not there on time.' Joe Jordan, who was a bit of a stickler for his rules, had set him a clear and early arrival time for the tasks he had to do. There was, of course, only one solution to this problem: we had to leave for the game at least a couple of hours earlier than we would otherwise have done to avoid Neil getting into trouble with Joe.

Stoke finished mid-table that season. After only five games of the following season, and, after less than a year in charge, Joe Jordan left in September 1994 following a thrashing at Bolton, and Lou Macari made a dramatic return to the club from Celtic.

Just before Christmas an away game at Tranmere Rovers' Prenton Park featured another memorable event in Neil's Stoke City career, which Lou Macari recounted in his autobiography, *Football, My Life*. Evidently before the game, when the players were stripping off, Martin Carruthers was showing off a new pair of boxer shorts and boasting how he had spent £60 on them.

NEIL

When the players went off, Lou told me to put on Martin's £60 silk underpants. This wasn't easy as I was a lot bigger than Martin. Lou then told me to put all the players' underpants on. So for an hour-and-a-half I had about thirteen pairs on. It was a real squeeze.

It was a marvellous night for Martin because he scored the only goal in a 1–0 win. When the team came back into the dressing room, they were all cheering because we had won the game. Martin got out of the bath and when he couldn't find his pants he shouted out, 'Some Scouse bastard's nicked my silk underpants.' I tried to keep a straight face but the other staff knew what I'd done and were all falling about with laughter.

MALCOLM

Lou said, 'They didn't last long, Martin, those sixty-quid pants of yours.' One by one the rest of the team climbed out of the bath only to discover that *their* underpants had disappeared, too. As Lou described it, 'The players genuinely thought that some weirdo had been through their things stealing footballers' pants.'

Neil revealed the truth by taking off his tracksuit. One by one they reclaimed their underpants to reveal that the pair on the bottom, next to Neil's skin, were Martin's expensive silk boxers.

Martin Carruthers wasn't very pleased:

> I had these new silk boxers, and the day before I'd been giving Nello some banter, and I came in and saw him wearing them, and when he saw me he scratched his balls with them and pulled them about and they were tearing, and Lou Macari was egging him on, so we dumped him in a cold bath.

NEIL

Martin Carruthers was very proud of his expensive boxer shorts, and Lou wanted to teach him a lesson. It was very funny to see their faces when they came back into the dressing room and couldn't find their underpants. They didn't all like it, but it was worth it. The main thing was that we had won the game that night. Martin Carruthers scored the goal, so me wearing his underpants was a lucky omen.

MALCOLM

Neil's relationship with Lou was more than just a work-related thing. Neil could be a bit of a confidant for Lou. I think that worked because Neil had no agenda other than just doing his best for the guy who had given him a chance to work at his beloved club. They used to walk Lou's dog together, but Neil also walked the dog for him, sometimes around the training ground.

NEIL

Once I lost the dog. I was really worried what Lou would say, but, fortunately for me, the dog found its own way home. I was very happy that I hadn't lost it for good.

MALCOLM

Mike Sheron arrived from Norwich City in November 1995:

> Nello was a character. There was always banter and it lifted the spirits when he came into the dressing room. Everything was focused on Nello rather than thinking about the game. He was a happy-go-lucky guy. He was good to have around. I'd heard stories about things going too far in the past, but it certainly didn't happen when I was there. There were one or two comments but Nello would always tell them if they were out of order. Winnie was lovely. She couldn't go in the dressing room, so Nello did. She was in the laundry.
>
> I'm a big Liverpool fan, so I called Nello 'Robbie' after Robbie Fowler and he called me 'Macca' after Steve McManaman. We still do that to this day.

NEIL

Macca is still a very good friend of mine and he plays for the Neil Baldwin Football Club. Of course, the real Robbie and the real Macca are very good friends of mine, and I had my picture taken with them and a group of other players when I went to see them when they played for Manchester City. I recently had a sportsman's evening with Robbie in Stoke, at which George Andrews was the compère, and he interviewed me on stage. Robbie was very pleased to meet up with me again.

MALCOLM

One of the incidents recalled by reporter George Andrews, who then worked at Radio Stoke, at that evening was his own kidnapping at a game against rivals Port Vale. George was there to represent the Vale viewpoint on air, whilst Nigel Johnson, an iconic figure among Stoke fans who still does the commentaries, was there to give the Stoke City perspective. They were due to share the commentary.

Nigel recalls: 'George was due to do the first shift, but kick-off arrived and he was nowhere to be seen, so I had to fill in. He eventually arrived looking very flustered to tell me he'd been kidnapped by Nello and others.'

George takes up the story:

> Lou always allowed the local media in areas in which you would not be allowed at other clubs. It was part of his style. A group of them led by Nello and Winnie had a pre-laid plan. They got me into the laundry, just down from Lou's office, tied me to a chair, put tape round my mouth, put a notice round my neck saying 'George is a Stoke fan' and locked the door. I couldn't get out, but

NEIL BALDWIN – MY STORY

was due to be upstairs to go on air. Eventually, I was able to make a noise which was heard by the physio who let me out. Nello thought it was hilarious and still talks about it to this day. I wouldn't be surprised if Lou was behind it. He used to wind Nello up about me, saying 'That George Andrews…' and get Nello to berate me.

NEIL

It was Lou's and Winnie's idea, and also John Rudge, who was at the Vale at that time. But it was only a joke. George is still a good friend of mine.

MALCOLM

He is indeed. Today George says:

> I have some great memories of Nello. Once we set up a race round the ground between him and Bernard Painting, the physio, with Nello given a big start, which was hilarious. You cannot but like him. He's a terrific guy who has made friends wherever he goes. He is welcome at Port Vale and Crewe and made friends at all the clubs Stoke City visited.
>
> Lou allowed the local media to go on the team coach and I have great memories of some of those trips, particularly if they involved overnight stays when Lou would open his box of tricks involving Nello in some joke or other. Once he arranged for a large wet fish to be left on Nello's pillow. But

he allowed him to get his own back on the team coach by walking round giving the players a clip round the face with this fish, until it disintegrated. Sadly, it just couldn't happen today.

It's amazing the way things have turned out for him, and you wonder how he got to certain places. Now he is just drawing on the warmth of the local people and the whole country, which is great.

MALCOLM

Lou's second spell at the club lasted for two-and-a-half years. A mid-table finish was followed by a play-off place when we lost over two legs to Leicester City, before it was back to mid-table in 1996–7, the last season at the Victoria Ground. The emotional last ever game at our historic home against West Bromwich Albion – the Baggies – also turned out to be Lou's last game in charge of Stoke City.

The Britannia Stadium was opened by Sir Stanley Matthews, who missed the goal when he was supposed to be symbolically putting the ball in the net. It was a bad omen for the season, which ended in relegation, made worse for many Stoke fans by the fact that Port Vale escaped relegation on the last day of the season. Stoke had three managers that season: Chic Bates, Chris Kamara, who won only one game out of fourteen, and Alan Durban.

But, throughout all this, Neil was a constant, looking after the kit and trying to keep the players amused in a disastrous season.

NEIL

That first season at the new ground was shocking. I don't know what the players were playing at. Of course, I'd known Chic for years as he was already at the club. He was very nice to me. Chris Kamara was very happy with me, too, and, when we played at Oxford in March, he let me leave the team hotel to go and watch the circus.

Alan Durban was also OK. But it didn't do any good having three different managers. I offered to take on the manager's job but they didn't take me up on it. They would have won more games if I had been manager.

CHAPTER SIX

MORE TIME TO SPEND AT KEELE AND LOOKING AFTER MUM

NEIL

While I was Stoke City kit man, my mum was getting quite frail, and had to go to hospital for long periods. Stoke signed the Welsh international goalkeeper Neville Southall for the last couple of months of the season in 1998. Neville had been one of the best goalkeepers in the world, though he was getting a bit old when he came to play for us. In fact he was the third-oldest player ever to play for Stoke City.

When I was away because we were playing at Reading, my mum was taken to hospital. I was really worried and kept trying to ring the hospital to find out how she was, but I couldn't get through.

Big Neville Southall asked me what was wrong. After I told him, he went away and came back with enough money for a taxi to take me all the way back to Stoke, which was a lot of money. I told him he didn't need to do that and that I couldn't afford to pay him back. He said, 'Don't worry about that, Nello. I don't want the money back. That doesn't matter. The only thing that matters is that you should get back to Stoke as quickly as possible to see your mum, so go and get that taxi.' And I did. I have never forgotten how kind he was to me that day. I don't forget good people like that.

Most of the players were very nice to me. There are too many to mention them all. Peter Thorne was another player who was always very kind to me, and gave me some money sometimes. Andy Griffin was always very friendly to me. He was an exciting young full-back who was sold to Newcastle United a month after Southall arrived. After he had left Stoke I went up to Newcastle to see him. I rang up to tell him I was coming. He met me at the club and took me to his house. He said I could stay for a few days, so I did. I met the striker Alan Shearer while I was there, so he became a very good friend of mine.

As Mum got older and not so well, I had to do more to look after her, but I didn't mind because she had been such a good mother to me. We were a good team, like Stoke City. She taught me how to look after myself. Les and Mary Bailey are very good friends and helped us a lot.

MALCOLM

Neil was by now very well established in his flat, getting by with more than a little help from his friends – and his mum. Mary was trying to prepare for the day when she might not be around or at least could not cope so well. She became friends with Les and Mary Bailey, who were to play a significant role in Mary's and Neil's lives. Mary recalls:

> We first met Mary in 1993 through the Christadelphian church and became very good friends. When we first knew her, Neil was already in his flat. She had originally done all Neil's shopping, but then she took Neil shopping with her, and eventually found she needed him with her. Finally, she gave him a list and he did the shopping. He slowly took it over and it was fascinating to watch, to the point where one day we remember him saying, 'What about some of that fresh fish like we had last week?' and 'I will get in some bacon.'

Les adds:

> Neil came to us with his problems. Once he had a huge fuel bill from Npower. He had been with Midlands Electricity but someone persuaded him to change – we suspect it was a salesman at the door. He had been buying fuel stamps and the lady at the post office knew how much he had to put in, but after he had changed to Npower, they had been estimating his bills for over a year.
>
> Neil didn't understand about estimating at all and kept saying that he had been paying enough at the post office but Npower couldn't care two hoots about the problem. We got through to

somebody; they just said, we must have Mr Baldwin there before we talk to you. Eventually we managed to get Neil there at an agreed time to start to sort it out.

Then there was another big incident. Neil read the meter, but he got two digits the wrong way round with the result that a bill came in for over two thousand pounds. I don't know why computers let these ridiculous bills go out.

Mary had a solicitor from Market Drayton to look after her affairs and set up a trust fund for Neil and the church after she had gone. The solicitor never wanted to charge for her visits, so Mary always used to take a sponge cake to the solicitor.

NEIL

That business with the electricity bills upset me because Mum always brought me up not to be in debt. I had been doing my best to pay the proper amount at the post office. They should have known that I must have made a mistake reading that meter. Anybody can do that. Malcolm makes mistakes and forgets things all the time.

MALCOLM

My family were friends with Mary as well as Neil. They came to visit us in Sale. I remember the look of shock on the face of my youngest daughter, Lisa, on one occasion in our car when she was a young teenager and Neil announced, 'One of my birds has had a baby' – until it dawned that he was talking about the feathered variety. Lisa wrote letters to Mary and has unearthed a couple of Mary's replies from May 1998, when Lisa was aged fifteen.

May 19th 1998

Dear Lisa

Please forgive me for not writing sooner. I meant to before you finished your exams for I expect they are over now. I hope so, so you can enjoy this lovely weather. This suits me fine. Anyone with heart trouble feels a different person. It is the warm air. It is really wonderful to feel as well as I am. One gets a different outlook.

And I'm pleased for Neil. He is enjoying tidying up his flat (in his way I expect) and comes to me for lunch. Then on to Keele. My friends come tomorrow for the fortnightly clean to change his bed etc.

He went to the meeting at Stoke last night. Brian Little [Stoke manager] was guest speaker. It was held in the ground with it being so nice. It said on Radio Stoke there were 500 fans there. No Moxey, Coates or Humphries and he [Brian] is seeing about [Danny] Tiatto, I think that's how you spell it, joining the squad. He told Neil to report for work July 1st. It's earlier than expected. Neil is a bit sorry I think but he's having 2 whole weeks in Cambridge and the last weekend [in

June] at Lichfield where he goes each yr. It's nice company for me to see him every day and he sees to Jess [the dog].

Now dear I hope you'll accept this little present. I don't bother with much jewellery now, so want you to accept this for your very kind thoughts to me. I was so taken up when you came to the hospital with Dad. It really made my day seeing you both and it's all thanks to dear Neil that I know you all.

The chain is real gold and I bought the pearl a year or so ago to brighten it up. Of course you may not wear it. I don't know what young teenagers like but it is just a thought Lisa. Enjoy your outing on Sat. with Dad. Love to mum, Zoe and Zara also Dad of course. My love and best wishes especially to you.

From
Mary and Neil x x

The friends coming to clean Neil's flat and change his bed were Les and Mary Bailey. We had been to see her in hospital. Her heart condition was causing her some difficulty. Brian Little had been appointed as the new manager of Stoke City but, as we shall see, things didn't work out for Neil under the new regime in the way Mary and Neil were anticipating.

The Saturday outing referred to was to see England v. Saudi Arabia in a 'warm-up' game at Wembley, prior to the World Cup that summer. The game turned out to be a boring goal-less draw, as Mary notes in her next letter after Lisa sent her a match programme. The letter gives more detail on the support Neil was by now giving to his mum.

May 31st 1998

Dear Lisa

What a thoughtful young lady you are. I can't say thank you enough. How delightful of you to send me your special programme. I was thrilled Lisa but now I have read it you must have it back in memory of the occasion, although it didn't sound a very thrilling game but just to be there with the atmosphere must have been quite an experience. Neil wasn't interested in that game Lisa. It's the proper one he likes at the end of the season.

I'm so pleased for you that your exams are over. Now you can relax and look forward to a holiday. This next week will be Neil's 4th week on his holiday at home then next Mon. June 8th he hopes to go to Cambridge for 2 weeks then he has a week and 3 days till he start[s] work on July 1st.

He has enjoyed being at his flat Lisa. He says 'it's his own' but he's a fabulous son. He has come at 7.30 every morning to take Jessie, but then he goes back to bed and gets up about 11 a.m. and has been coming to me for lunch. I'm really tired now Lisa for we both have salads but it takes me ages to

131

get both ready, as I am just beginning to get meals, as my friends have been preparing for me. I have no energy in the winter, but now I'm on these new tablets they really are great. Neil then goes to Keele at 2.30pm. Then comes home at 8.30pm to take Jess for her last walk. I am able to take her in the afternoon. My walking is improving Lisa which is a good thing, for I will be taking Jess 4 times per day but am looking forward to it.

It will be a nice change to be on my own. No washing or ironing for Neil for 2 weeks. It will be a real holiday for me Lisa and if the weather is not too hot I can take Jess sometimes in the car. Anything to get out of the house although I have a lovely back garden and am busy putting bedding plants in. It is good therapy for me Lisa. I can relax. It's a real joy to me. I like things just so. It does not matter how long it takes and when the weather is nice its good to sit in nice surroundings. Jess likes being in the garden like me.

Well dear friend I will close now. Excuse the scribble near the end but I am tired now it's 5.45pm so am going to have my tea. Please give my love to Dad and Mum and your 2 sisters also the lovely horse. We have 4 horses in the field on Gallowstree Lane by Keele roundabout. It's on a hill and I can see them from my window with my Binocs. They have had 1 foal each. What a joy it's given me to be able to see them. Neil took his camera. It cost him £6. He's a lovely boy, but they are good pictures.

Cheerio dear. I am delighted you like your little gift. When its appreciated its worth giving it away. Bye

Love from
Mary, Neil and Jessie x x x

NEIL

Then something happened at Stoke City that was upsetting. Before the start of the 1998–9 season, when Brian Little took over as manager, Jez Moxey, the chief executive, called me into his office, gave me a cup of tea, and told me that I was no longer needed at the club. I was very upset, because I loved my job. But after a little while I decided not to worry about it, but just carry on doing all the other things I like. You just have to get on with life. It gave me a lot more time to look after Mum and go up to Keele.

MALCOLM

Seventeen years on, Jez Moxey had no clear recollection of exactly why that decision was taken or who instigated it but told me that he would definitely not have done that unless the manager had asked for it or at the very least was happy with it, and that the Board were too.

NEIL

The following year another very good friend of mine, Kevin Keegan, became England manager. He was a great player. I once visited him at his house in Southampton when he played for Southampton in the early 1980s and I was down there with the circus. After he became England manager in 1999, he used to get me tickets when England played at Wembley.

MALCOLM

I remember telling some Stoke City friends about Neil's friendship with Kevin Keegan. They didn't really believe me. Then, after a game at the Britannia Stadium (I think it may have been the FA Cup game against Newcastle United in January 2008, just before Keegan went back for his second spell as Newcastle manager) we were all walking past the main entrance foyer, and there was Keegan sitting down with his arm round Neil. They believed me then.

Around this time Neil also got a further honour from the Keele Students' Union at a ceremony I attended along with Mike Sheron and one or two other Stoke players.

Mike recalls: 'My wife and I went up to Keele for the opening of Baldwin's Bar when they named one of the bars in the Students' Union after him, which was very appropriate, given how long he had been going there.'

NEIL

It was great to have that bar named after me. Quite a few players came to the ceremony, as well as Malcolm and a lot of my friends. I was really sorry when they changed it to something else many years later. That sometimes happens with students. One group leaves and the new ones do something else. They should always take my advice. After all, I've got a lot of experience up at Keele, and I'm older and wiser than they are. Maybe now I am even more famous, they will name the bar or something else in the union after me again.

MALCOLM

Peter Whieldon, who twenty years previously as a child had played football with Neil in Horwood Hall, was by now visiting Keele on business. He recalls:

> I was working for Imperial Tobacco and had to visit the Keele shop. I was astonished to see Neil sitting there in his chair in the Students' Union dressed as Father Christmas. His very first words were, 'Peter, can you get me a half of beer?' It was as though I had never left. He's just a fixture in the union. After that I saw him every Christmas.

NEIL

It's always marvellous when my old friends come back to Keele. They all want to see me because they know I won't be far away. Peter is a lovely lad, just like his mum and dad were. They looked after the students, just like I do. I was very sad when Peter's father Harold died in 2012. I went with Malcolm and Lesley to his funeral, where it was good to see both Peter and his older brother Tony again.

MALCOLM

Jonathan Hughes recalls his early encounters with Neil as a student at Keele in the late 1990s, when, for a while, he harboured hopes that Neil might be able help him with furthering his own football career:

I studied physiotherapy at the university between 1997 and 2000. From the age of eight I was a member of Oldham Athletic Centre of Excellence and in 1995 was offered a YTS at the club, which, on the instruction of my parents, I turned down to continue with my studies.

Whilst representing Stockport Boys town team I played alongside Dean Crowe, who, whilst I was at Keele, was starting to make a name for himself at Stoke. [Dean Crowe was a young Stoke striker who broke into the Stoke team in the 1997–8 season.]

Still harbouring hopes to make it in the game, one of my mates mentioned that there was 'a bloke' who worked at Keele who was linked to Stoke. That 'bloke' turned out to be Neil.

I first bumped into Neil in the leisure centre one evening after a five-a-side game in the Keele University league. I remember playing pretty well that evening and whilst speaking with Neil was thinking that he might have been down there doing a bit of scouting for Stoke and had been secretly impressed by my performance.

Though I don't recall that particular conversation in detail, what I do recall is the constant name-dropping. Apparently (according to Neil) he was second in line for the England job when [Glen] Hoddle was appointed. I remember thinking, That can't be right. But he did sound very convincing.

There were obviously lots of references to Lou and Stoke and also his own team, which he managed. Neil went on to tell me that his team played league clubs' reserve teams.

I must admit, I was a little unsure as to whether to believe Neil. However, as I was young and naïve, and still a little focused on making it in the game, I gave Neil the benefit of the doubt and agreed to turn out for his team one Sunday morning.

There had been no training sessions and I was a little in the dark as to the standard and whether I'd be able to cut it at the 'high level'. Still, I thought, if I put in a decent performance Neil would put in a word with the manager at Stoke and I might get a chance of going down to do a few sessions and meet up with my old mate Dean and hopefully impress.

Sunday came and I turned up at the steps of the Union at 9.30 as directed by Neil. The evening before, I'd stayed in to get a decent night's sleep whilst my mates had gone out to the Golfers (which at that time was pretty bouncing on Saturday nights).

There were only one or two lads there in addition to Neil. I think I was making a bit of small talk with one of the lads I had just met when Neil's boots caught my attention. Pretty much simultaneously I heard Neil telling one of the lads, he'd be playing centre-mid. He was talking up his game as if he was Hoddle in his prime.

This, in addition to the fact that there was no sign of our coach arriving to take us to the venue and a grand total of five players including Neil meant that I was now having serious doubts as to whether Neil would be my ticket to Stoke City.

A few minutes later, Neil advised us that he'd just been told the game had been cancelled. I went back to my halls at Barnes, tail between legs.

Following that day there were no further appearances for Neil's team, just the ad hoc meetings with Neil as I bumped into him around the campus. Usually the conversation would be me listening and Neil doing most of the talking.

NEIL

If Jon had stuck with it, I might have been able to make a footballer out of him and got him a trial at Stoke.

MALCOLM

Another Keele student of the time, also called Jon, paid a return visit to the campus after leaving, and found himself sharing an awkward moment with Neil. Everyone concerned was rather embarrassed, except, of course, Neil.

Here's his story:

As an ex-NBFC player and a director (I think all NBFC players become directors, not that there has ever been a single board meeting – in Neil's NBFC programme, the list of directors takes up about three pages), Neil was keen to introduce me to the new crop of players who had joined since I left. So he took me on his usual rounds around all the halls, being introduced to the new students. I listened to the familiar lines: 'That's a nice-looking jar of curry sauce on your shelf – that'd be lovely with a few chips'; and the disbelieving look on the student's face that was once my own.

About halfway round, we called at a room in the Oaks [a students' residence] and in his normal manner Neil hammered on the door and then tried to open it without waiting for a reply. The door didn't open, so Neil knocked again. Again no reply. We were about to walk away when Neil said that he thought he'd heard something and there was someone in the room after all.

It had already occurred to me that there were going to be people who, for whatever reason, didn't want to be disturbed, as it was at least 10 p.m., so I tried to encourage Neil to forget it and go on to the next place. But, alas, he was determined. There then followed a conversation, something like this.

Neil: 'Rob, Rob, are you there?'

No reply

Me: 'Come on, Neil, let's go. Even if he *is* there he doesn't want to be disturbed.'

Neil: 'Are you there, Rob?' (Hammers on door again.)

From the room: 'Umm, what is it, Neil?' (Very feeble voice, guilty and awkward-sounding.)

Neil: 'I knew you were there. Open up, I've got one of my old players to meet you.'

Rob: 'Could it wait till tomorrow, Neil? It's a bit awkward now.'

Neil: 'No, he'll be gone tomorrow. Open up. We won't keep you long.'

Me: 'No, Neil. I'll meet him next time I'm visiting. It's not convenient now.'

Neil: 'Come on, Rob.' (More hammering.)

Rob (swearing under his breath, quick movements occurring in room): 'Well, just to say hello, then, Neil. It's not convenient now.'

Me (to Rob): 'It's OK, I'll meet you next time. Come on, Neil.' (I attempt to physically drag Neil away – no easy task.)

Neil: 'It's all right, he said he doesn't mind.'

At this point we hear the lock open and the door open a fraction. A worried-looking lad with a red face appears at the door, dressed only in a towel around his waist.

Neil: 'Rob this is Jon, Jon this is Rob.'

Rob and Me: 'Pleased to meet you.' (We shake hands and Rob nearly loses his towel.)

Neil: 'Right, then, Rob, let's talk football tactics. You can cook us some of that lovely chilli con carne you did the other night – that was lovely.' (A worried look appears on Rob's face.)

Me (winking at Rob): 'It's OK Neil, I've got to get back now, anyway. I've met Rob. Now we can go on.'

Neil: 'OK, then.'

Neil turns away, saying goodbye. Relief starts to spread visibly over Rob's face. Then Neil remembers something and turns back.

Neil: 'Hey, Rob, show Jon that Spurs shirt you've got signed by all the players.'

Rob: 'Umm, it's not here, Neil.'

Neil: 'Yes it is. I saw it yesterday.' (Tries to worm his way past Rob, who stands firm.)

Rob: 'Well, it's a bit awkward, Neil. You see, I've got company.'

Neil: 'That's all right. Introduce us. Maybe he could sign up for NBFC.'

Rob: 'No, Neil. Umm, it's female company.'

Me (almost shouting): 'Come on, Neil, time to go.'

Neil: 'Oh, that's OK, Rob. Introduce us anyway. I promise not to talk about football too much. [Neil shouts into the room.] All right, duck?'

An embarrassed and annoyed female voice from the room says, 'Hello.'

By this stage four or five people, mainly in dressing gowns, have gathered in the corridor due to all the noise. Most of them are smirking.

Neil: 'Get the kettle on, then, Rob, and let's see that Spurs shirt.'

Without warning, Neil makes an attempt to open the door and catches Rob off guard. He succeeds in fully opening the door, where we see the poor girl desperately trying to cover every inch of herself in the duvet. Whispers start in the corridor. It appears this isn't the girl who should have been there.

Rob makes a desperate and all-too-late lunge to close the door and in his efforts the towel falls off completely. He desperately lunges for the towel but trips up over Neil's leg and ends up in the corridor stark naked. People have gathered and the smirks have turned to riotous laughter.

Neil: 'Well, *there's* something you don't see every day. Anyway, Rob, we'll get off now, then.'

Rob crawls back into his room and locks the door. A big argument gets going in the room as we leave.

Neil (to me as we are leaving): 'He's a nice lad, Rob, but I don't know what got into him tonight. He wasn't himself. Anyway, I want you to meet Chris next...'

Back on the campus road, the silhouette of two people can be seen in one room throwing things at each other. Neil's eyesight isn't perfect.

Neil: 'That's Rob's room, look, he's waving at us. [Neil waves up at the room.] He's all right really. I'll put him in the team for next week. See, I look after all my players.'

But that was only one side of Neil's relationship with the students. Sometimes he could help when no one else could. He once talked a young female student out of committing suicide. It is a measure of the nature of the relationship that she confided in Neil. On her graduation day her parents thanked Neil for what he had done.

NEIL

I told her that we all have to go sometime, but why go now? And just think how your parents will feel if you do this.

142

But in 1999 something really awful happened. Lou's son Jonathan committed suicide. I got on well with him. I thought he was the best footballer out of the three Macari boys. I prayed for Lou and his family and Jonathan. I still do.

MALCOLM
Lou referred to this in an article in *The Sunday Times* in June 2015:

> Life can be tough. It was tough for Neil. It's tough for everyone at some stage. I've a great picture of Neil sitting on a bench with my boy. Neil is wearing a Ninja Turtle outfit. My lad was just there because we had brought him along to the game. At that time he would have been about sixteen. He got on well with Neil; Neil got on well with him.

This is a good indication of the very close personal bond which existed, and still exists to this day, between Lou and his family and Neil. It is much deeper than that between a manager and a kit man.

NEIL
Of course, in 2000, I'd been coming to Keele for forty years. We had a great celebration for my forty years. We had a game between NBFC and the All Stars, which was refereed by Uriah Rennie, who was a very famous referee, and we also had a service of thanksgiving in the chapel and a party.

MALCOLM

I remember the game well. There was even a printed programme for it. I think it was done by the Students' Union. It even included a personal letter on FA headed paper sent to Neil's home address from the England manager Kevin Keegan:

14 January 2000

Dear Neil,

I was delighted to learn that special events are being organised for 12 March to help you celebrate your 40th year. It'll be a great day for you, and the team, and I hope the weather keeps fine for the All Stars match.

I have the honour of being the President of the Neil Baldwin Association Football Club and I send my very best wishes to all the present members, including the players of course.

This is a momentous year for all of us in football terms. I will be taking my England team to Belgium and Holland in the summer and will be hoping we can produce performances that will make the whole country proud of us.

With kind regards,
Kevin Keegan

My daughter Zara and I turned up after it had started. As we walked across the Keele playing fields we could see the game under way in the distance. I said to Zara, 'That ref looks a bit like Uriah Rennie.' As we got closer, I said, 'It *is* Uriah Rennie.'

Uriah at that time was one of the top referees in the country. This was extraordinary even by Neil's standards. I wondered whether Uriah had been misled about who exactly was playing in this game.

Nigel Johnson, a football commentator for BBC Radio Stoke, was there too, and he was as surprised as I was even though he'd been warned. 'Come and support my team Saturday, Nigel,' Neil had said to him. 'I've got Uriah Rennie reffing.' Nigel thought: 'Yes, and pigs will fly' but he turned up anyway to support Neil.

Nigel knew Neil well from long before Neil became Stoke City kit man. Before Stoke matches Nigel would do vox pops in the radio van at the entrance to the ground, getting fans to give their opinions. Some fans went shy, or couldn't get their opinions out, but when he saw Neil, he always knew it was going to be all right. 'Neil loved to pontificate, he loved to be there, he enjoyed the limelight, and if he disagreed with you he'd say so. He was a very good interviewee, always ready with an answer but economical with words.'

That day, as Nigel walked towards the pitch, I thought, 'I don't believe it, that IS Uriah Rennie.'

Uriah is indeed a very good friend of Neil's. He explains how their friendship started, how he came to be refereeing the game and his view of Neil:

I first met Neil when I was a Football League linesman. When I was officiating at Stoke he was always there outside the entrance.

From 1998 onwards I was a Premier League referee. Once, we did some training sessions at Keele University, including refereeing some tournaments which were on there. Neil watched our training sessions. You could tell he was genuine and approachable.

We went for a walk, but because we were not geography students we got lost and ended up in the Students' Union. Neil was there and he came to talk to us. When we were walking around, we didn't carry any money but we ended up having a few beers in the union. I think this is because Neil had got other students and other people to buy the drinks. In fact, I'm not sure I can ever remember seeing Neil going to a bar.

He told me he had got this team who would be playing a big game and would I referee it? I said that if I'm in the country I'll do it. When I got onto the International list, he always seemed to know my appointments and when I was going to Europe. I don't know how he knew this because it was before the widespread use of the Internet.

But, once I say I'll do something, I make sure I do. Neil did tell me that some big personalities would be there and playing. But it's important to understand that those people weren't the driver to me agreeing to do it. After all I was refereeing superstars anyway every week.

I did it because of Neil, because I class him as a friend and an inspiration, because he continues to do all that he does. People do not always understand the relationship we have. Talking about his so-called disabilities, it's all about ability, not *dis*ability. It's about friendship and having a very positive attitude.

He displays focus, determination and a will to succeed, no matter how small or large the task. If he says, 'I will phone X' he goes away and does it. He displays such a positive attitude to life and its challenges. This is something I want to pass on to my little ones. He's a great model for anyone, regardless of whether they have any disability or not, in chasing his goals. You couldn't put a cash amount on the influence he's had on my conscience and my commitment to help worthwhile causes. Others like me give what's a little bit to them, but it's a lot to him.

He's been at Keele all these years and every year he has to re-evaluate and change his relationships because the students change, and create new relationships, but he does that very well.

I remember driving across from Sheffield for that game and, when I got there, wandering around to find it. I got changed and had my boots in my hand. The students were all very jovial, saying, 'What are *you* doing here? How has Neil got you to do this?' Neil had promised that he would get me two linesmen – or assistant referees, as we call them nowadays. But, when I arrived, it turned out to be two of his squad players who weren't playing, his mates; he just told them that they were to be assistant referees.

MALCOLM

One of those linesmen was Peter Whieldon, who, as we have seen, had played football with Neil as a child, and encountered him as Father Christmas years later in the union. He recalls:

> I heard about the game and turned up to watch. Neil saw me and just told me to run the line. At the end of the game Uriah gave a dubious penalty. I think it was to give Neil the chance to score, which he did, although I think the kick had to be retaken a couple of times after Neil had missed because the keeper was supposed to be off his line. He didn't seem to make much of an effort to save the one which went in, and Neil turned round in celebration with his elbow bent and his finger in the air.

NEIL

Not many keepers save my penalties if they obey the rule and stay on their line. A good referee like Uriah will always spot one who doesn't.

The service of thanksgiving for my forty years was taken

by my good friend Keith Sutton, the Bishop of Lichfield. Just as for my thirty-years' service, Malcolm and Steve Botham were both there again, but this time they were talking in the service about my life, which was marvellous. It was another lovely service.

MALCOLM

Neither Steve nor I had realised that the other was going to be there and we had the same role. Neil had forgotten to mention it to either of us, so we had to exchange notes hastily to make sure we weren't just duplicating each other in what we said.

In the vestry with the Bishop as the service was about to start, I said to Steve, 'The last time we met was at the last one of these.' The Bishop turned round slightly sharply to enquire, 'You mean there've been other services for Neil?'

'Yes,' we said, this being the third. It was clear that Neil had also forgotten to tell this to the Bishop, whose look seemed to indicate that, while perhaps he thought one service for Neil was fine, the idea of three might be excessive. But it was far too late. The service was about to start, and it went fine, including the obligatory Neil solo. Neil, as ever, revelled in the occasion, and it was clear, as it always is, just how much the chapel community at Keele love him.

Les and Mary Bailey were also there, and Mary recalls: 'The students did a play in honour of Neil's birthday. An elderly Church Army lady came all the way from Clacton in Essex just for that service. We have a lovely memory of the Bishop sitting on a bench with Neil eating an ice-cream.'

NEIL

In 2001 I applied for the England manager's job, but they gave it to him with the glasses, Sven-Göran Eriksson.

Because I have been at Keele so long, I have a very long list of former students who are very good friends of mine. Sometimes they come back to Keele for reunions, and I love to see them. I go to the reunion dinners and I see a lot of my old friends there.

MALCOLM

Once upon a time, the establishment didn't quite approve of Neil's being at the dinner. Jo Rogers, a former Keele student who married lecturer John Rogers, used to organise the reunion dinners, and recalls:

> I was secretary to the Keele Society for many years. Each year I would organise the Keele Society Reunion weekend and, as the date approached, Neil would contact me, checking on the date and which groups were invited back. On the evening of the dinner, Neil would be there, at first just mingling with the graduates and clearly expecting to have a place at the meal, which, of course, I found for him. He enjoyed it, the graduates were delighted (or sometimes bemused if they were of a pre-Neil era).
>
> But in the early 1990s it all became much more professional. The university appointed a lady with overall responsibility for dealings with alumni. The reunion dinners were still organised by me. Neil still made an appearance and enjoyed his free

dinner amongst friends, but our arrangement was unpopular to say the least. I suspect she felt Neil had no place at such events and I got reprimanded severely for allowing it. Not that it made a jot of difference to me, nor to Neil, who never realised that he was ever unwelcome, bless him.

The dinners are now organised by John Easom. He says:

When I took over alumni relations in 2005 at first I also bridled at Neil inviting himself to reunions unannounced. But at the time I knew neither the Man nor the Myth. After a couple of years I understood and let him attend if he wanted to – invariably free of charge. Some things just don't fit into rule books.

CHAPTER SEVEN

NEIL LEARNS TO LIVE ON HIS OWN

NEIL

Even though I was sad to see it, it was God's will and best for Mum that she went into a home, because she couldn't cope, even though I was doing my best to help her. It was on Keele Road, a very short distance from her house and my flat, which was very helpful for me in visiting her and doing errands for her. It was a lovely home and she was happy there.

MALCOLM

Around the turn of the century Mary was getting increasingly frail. In some ways it was a blessing in disguise that Neil had left his job at Stoke City, otherwise he would have been able to give her much less help and support than he did.

She eventually moved into Thistleberry House, a local-authority care home, in 2002. Her beloved dog, Jessie, had died before she moved into the home. Les and Mary Bailey had given her much support. Les recalls:

> Towards the end Mary was in and out of hospital for eighteen months to two years. The year before she went into the home she had had more weeks in hospital than she had at home. We had to sort things out with the carers. They only made soup and toast. They were supposed to be there for forty-five minutes but they weren't.
>
> Once, we found out that she hadn't been paid her pension for six months, but she hadn't noticed. She used to give Neil money to do the shopping and one day got worried that she hadn't got enough money. This was because nobody had responsibility for notifying the pension authority that somebody had come out of hospital. At first they refused to back-date it.
>
> One day we found a gas ring on in her house. On another occasion paper was singeing close to the gas ring. It was a close shave. She was no longer able to cook meals. Neil started to get very good at helping his mum, although he still couldn't tie his shoelaces!

Mary adds:

> We went to her eightieth birthday party in the home. She also had her eighty-first birthday

party there. She was in the residential home for about eighteen months. She was very happy there, despite the lack of independence, because it had got to the point where she could no longer cope at home. She always had a tremendous sense of humour. Visiting her was never a burden.

We found a building society book in Neil's name with six hundred pounds. Mary said that you are going to have to give it to him. A few months later there was no money in it. We asked him why there was no money and realised that he had little concept of adding things up. We got in touch with [the mental-health charity] MIND about Neil's welfare, and social services went round to see him. He simply told them that he didn't have a problem and that was the end of that.

Vic Trigg remembers: 'Mary became progressively more forgetful in later life and by the time she was living in the care home she could not remember the names of visitors when it was time to say goodbye to them.'

That was my experience, too, as she couldn't remember the names of my three daughters or got them mixed up. Although she had been getting more frail and forgetful, it was unexpected when she died overnight shortly before Christmas 2003. Neil rang to give us the news. It was one of the saddest phone calls I have ever received, because she was not only a close friend, but a truly remarkable woman.

NEIL

Of course, I was very sad when Mum died. Even though it is God's will and I know she has gone to a better place, I cried. But you have to get on with life. I knew that she wouldn't want me to be sad, so I decided not to be. She is up there watching me.

MALCOLM

The funeral was held on 2 January 2004, in the Christadelphian Hall on Dimsdale Parade, Newcastle. It was an icy day. We had been away for New Year in remote Mid Wales and had to drive back through some snow and ice that morning to get there. We only just made it. It was a very simple ceremony, which was conducted by Les Bailey. Neil gave a eulogy to his mum, which was simple and beautiful. Les recalls: 'I wanted to prepare the ground, by not asking Neil to say anything if he was upset. But he was quite OK.'

NEIL

I said what a good mum she had always been to me; how she had always looked after me; how she tried to keep me healthy by giving me salads and how she had let me go off to the circus and always let me do whatever I wanted to do. It was sad, of course, but I wasn't nervous. I never am.

MALCOLM

Vic Trigg recalls: 'We were all concerned at the funeral about Neil's future, even though we all knew that he had built up a wide collection of friends and adds to them all the time.'

Les and Mary Bailey had a quiet word with Vic and Helen, who said that they would 'take Neil on'.

When Mary was in the residential home, Neil spent Christmas Day with her, apart from going to chapel at Keele. Since her death, Tony and Irene Bartlett have invited him to their house for Christmas Day. They drive from Congleton to Keele to pick him up after church. Tony says:

> Neil always wants to watch the Queen, and always asks me to get him some circus programmes off eBay.
>
> A few years ago he said that a student from Nigeria called Joshua had nowhere to go on Christmas Day, and could he join us? He's not afraid to ask the direct question and forces you to make a choice between the kind and Christian thing to do, or the more selfish thing. These choices make you a kinder person. How can you say no?
>
> In 2013 Joshua was going somewhere else at Christmas. Neil then said that he had an Egyptian friend who had nowhere to go, so could he replace Joshua? That's the true spirit of Christmas. Neil challenges your Christianity in the nicest possible way.

NEIL

I don't like to think of anyone having nowhere to go at Christmas. It sometimes happens at Keele for students and staff who have come from abroad. There are more of them than there used to be. After all, the Christmas story is about having room at the inn. Tony and Irene are very kind people to welcome us on Christmas Day.

In 2004 Tony and Vic built a lovely new aviary for all my birds in my flat. Before that they flew freely around the flat. That was nice but they made a bit of a mess. I had a cleaner who left because of the mess. So it's better that they are all now in a proper aviary and cages.

MALCOLM

Neil has his supporting cast. At home as well as Vic and Helen and Tony and Irene, this includes Laurence and Jenny Wood, health professionals who are members of the Keele chapel and have helped Neil manage his hip replacement and diabetes, as well as organising both voluntary, and employed domestic and health, support.

Jenny says:

> Neil first met Laurence at Keele chapel in 1999. I didn't know Laurence then. When I visited his house, I was amazed by all these clothes drying around the place, until Laurence explained that he does the washing for a friend of his, and started to explain about Neil. But I think he attracts the right people.

Neil's cleaner, Carrie Latham, does a fantastic job in challenging circumstances and says, 'If it was anyone other than Neil, I probably wouldn't do it.' Stephanie Kent helps Neil with shopping and looking after his birds. His old friends Terry and Sue Conroy have also provided valuable practical help tidying his flat and helping him acquire a new wardrobe, appropriate for the many invitations which have followed *Marvellous*.

NEIL

They look after me, and I look after them. That's what friends are for.

MALCOLM

Not all Neil's trips abroad were quite so straightforward as the one to Venice (which we dealt with in Chapter 5). Les Bailey recalls:

> On one occasion Neil went to visit a circus in Switzerland. Someone at Keele had organised flights and hotels. We asked him about money. When he told us what he was taking, we realised he only had a small amount of money per day. He didn't understand the concept of the exchange rate with Swiss currency, or how much things cost in Switzerland.
>
> Unfortunately, it didn't work out with the circus. He had booked in the hotel for a few days only. He thought after that he could stay in their circus caravans, but that didn't work out. He wanted to come back early because he couldn't get put up. We got a phone call from the Swiss airport people from Neil. He wanted to come home, but his ticket was a fixed one for a particular later date. He said, 'I've run out of money.' The airline eventually

booked him on an earlier flight and he said, 'Can
you pick me up from Manchester airport.'

On the same trip, he got lost. The Swiss police
picked him up and took him back to his hotel.

NEIL

I don't have any problems travelling abroad. I've been to
Switzerland, Denmark, Finland, Ireland and Germany.
There are always people who will help you. I am nice to
people and they are nice to me. If they are not, I'll find
people who are.

MALCOLM

Vic Trigg sums it up like this:

> The most remarkable thing about Neil is how
> other people treat him. His innocence seems to
> bring out the best in most people. He without
> doubt has guardian angels, who can be the most
> unlikely people. He sets off hitchhiking, or goes to
> visit a circus in Finland with minimal knowledge of
> where he's going or how to get there, yet has always
> escaped trouble, and is often helped by complete
> strangers. He goes to wait outside a theatre for
> Ken Dodd, who not only arrives and sees him,
> but gets him into the show for free. When his hip
> was particularly bad he took a fall on an escalator
> in Austria – behind him was a Lutheran pastor to
> pick him up.

NEIL

No, Vic hasn't got it right. It was in Germany, not Austria. I had asked one of the airport ladies to help me with my case on that escalator but she just ignored me, which was why I fell over. If she had helped me, I would have been OK. She was then told off by her boss for not helping me. I nearly always find that, if you ask for something, people give it to you.

MALCOLM

If you're Neil, that's generally true, though even with Neil it's not 100 per cent.

Mary Bailey recalls an occasion when it didn't work out the way Neil hoped:

> There was a Finnish lecturer at Keele called Aaro, who was over here for a year with his family. He was a lovely man who had visited Mary in hospital and had been taking Neil around and also visiting Mary at home.
>
> Mary told us that she and Neil were going to spend Christmas with them. She had asked Neil – are you sure, and he had said yes. But on Christmas Eve she rang us to say that Aaro's wife knew nothing about it and they hadn't been invited at all. So at the last minute they came to us for Christmas.
>
> Neil was very upset about it, but we felt he didn't really understand the difference between being invited and inviting yourself.
>
> Our son was at the grumpy teenage stage and we

wondered what he would make of Neil, but Neil just came in and said 'Hello Andy' as though he'd known him all his life and started to talk about football to him, so it was absolutely fine. He sat there most of the day doing a colouring book we bought for him.

He used to tell us about bishops he knew, Prince Philip etc. At first we thought it was all his imagination but eventually you realise that it's just all true. Mary had difficulty persuading him that he would not be able to go to university or become a vicar. But she had great determination that he would have a good life, and he certainly has.

NEIL

I met another old Keele friend about that time, and that's how the Neil Baldwin Cup started. That's a cup that football teams all over the country now compete for every March. It was all down to Neil Mosley, who had played in the NBFC when he was at Keele in the mid-1980s and had become head of sport at Imperial College, London. When he was a student we used to meet in the Students' Union and we'd say, 'Hallo, Neil'; 'Hallo, Neil.'

MALCOLM

Neil Mosley chairs the University Sports Directors' Network and gets to know his counterparts at other universities, one of whom is Angela Dale at Keele. After talking to Angela and her colleague Dennis Bourne about Neil, he thought he would like to see him again, and looked out for him the next time he had a chance to go to Keele.

'I went to see Angela and we went to the Sneyd Arms for lunch with Neil,' says Neil Mosley. In the Sneyd, the pub in Keele village, Neil Mosley said, probably only half seriously, 'I ought to get the Neil Baldwin Football Club playing a Neil Mosley Eleven from London.' He should have known that Neil would take him at his word. The match was soon arranged.

'My eleven were Imperial College people,' says Neil Mosley. 'We just got people together for the game, and played at the QPR training ground.' It became an annual event and eventually morphed into a competition for the Neil Baldwin Cup, with a motley collection of teams from all over the country competing. It's now five-a-side and held indoors every February, with eight to ten teams. There's no entry fee, Imperial College does the organisation and provides the space, and Neil Baldwin presents the trophy and makes a speech before everyone goes to the bar for some food and drink.

Neil Mosley says:

> The teams who come are mostly teams with which Neil has some sort of association. Downing College, Cambridge, generally supplies a team. Quite often a team is there because Neil knows the Anglican vicar. One time we somehow had Stuart Pearce there, when he was England under-21 manager. Neil must have fixed that. Neil just said to me, 'Stuart Pearce, he's a very good friend of mine.'

Neil Mosley does a wonderful Neil Baldwin imitation – even better than mine. He sums it up like this: 'No one ever says no to Neil. He can get people together to say yes.'

CHAPTER EIGHT

NEIL IN THE TWENTY-FIRST CENTURY: A TIME TO REAP

NEIL

In 2010 I celebrated fifty years at Keele. There was a party in the chapel, the NBFC played a match and there was a service of thanksgiving in the Keele University chapel, conducted by my old friend Jonathan Gledhill, the Bishop of Lichfield. It was a great honour to have Bishop Jonathan preaching, as I had known him ever since he came to Keele as a young undergraduate.

It was the fourth service of thanksgiving I have had at Keele. Not many people have had that, have they? It was good to have it in the university chapel because I have been worshipping there all these years. I always worship at Keele, including Christmas Day. I have known thirteen Anglican, fourteen Catholic and fifteen Methodist chaplains at Keele. They have all been very good to me. I help them with the services.

The students produced a bone-china commemorative mug to celebrate it. It has a picture of me wearing a mitre on it, because my nickname is the Bishop of Keele. George Jackson produced it in his workplace in Stoke. The Lichfield Diocesan magazine, called *Spotlight*, had an article about it and called me 'the new Bishop of Keele'. That was good, wasn't it?

MALCOLM

The same year, Neil had a hip replaced. His mobility had been deteriorating for some time. His friend Laurence Wood from the chapel persuaded Neil to get something done about it. Tony Bartlett recalls taking Neil a supply of coloured card and crayons in hospital, from which he produced a large number of handmade thank-you cards. The Bishop of Stafford, Geoff Annas, as well as the Keele chaplains visited him in hospital.

Bishop Geoff says:

> Like most clowns, I think Nello has quite a complex side to his nature.
>
> Like many others, I have my fair share of good stories: processing with other bishops down the nave of St Paul's Cathedral or Westminster Abbey and watching as everyone speaks to Neil as they pass by; or his birthday party, where he famously ranted against David Cameron for introducing university fees and getting the students at Keele into debt and then in the next breath questioned why the same prime minister had not yet given

him an OBE. But behind all of this I believe there is a very deep-thinking man who cares a great deal about others.

Perhaps one of the greatest challenges to a Christian (and indeed for a non-Christian too) is to fulfil the great command of Jesus to 'love one another'. Neil has managed to do this by treating all people exactly the same – irrespective of any of the usual things that others use to differentiate, like age or status. Neil simply accepts people as they are and in this provides food for thought for us all.

MALCOLM

Reverend Michael Harding, who was at St Paul's church, Newcastle-under-Lyme, from 1970 to 1999, and was the Rural Dean of Newcastle, has known Neil for more than forty years.

Neil asks me about clergy movements in North Staffs. Nowadays the diocesan diary is circulated to bishops, archdeacons – and to Neil. He phones me up every week (but daily for a few months after his mother died) to share his news.

He often provides reassurance to strangers. They know they have at least one friend rooting for them in a strange land, as with the lonely Keele University freshers or any newcomer who attends Keele University chapel, where he hands out the service books.

I once mentioned Neil in a sermon and afterwards a lady said that she'd known him when he was a teenager. Her mother, who lived just opposite the Stoke FC ground, had been employed as the 'official mother' to look after young footballers arriving from all parts of Britain. She recalled how Neil would regularly turn up at her mother's house for a cup of tea, and sit chatting to these newcomers so that they began to feel at home in the Potteries. I wonder whether Lou Macari knew that?

He always attended services when a new vicar was installed, to welcome them to the area, but now he also makes up an individual prayer card which he gives to everyone who is ordained deacon or priest in the Lichfield diocese, welcoming them to their new role in life, reminding them of their tasks and assuring them that he will continue praying for them.

He's taken to attending the services when a priest is consecrated as a bishop, welcoming them to their new role and presenting his prayer card for them too. I gather that bishops in procession, say in Westminster Abbey, are inclined to bow to him as they pass, or even give him a wink.

At Keele, whether you're a brilliant footballer or wouldn't get into the university teams, there's a welcome to enjoy a game through Neil's team, playing against other institutions, Oxford and Cambridge colleges, theological colleges, and sometimes even professionals. It's reassuring to know that you don't have to be a star footballer to enjoy the game.

Neil, says Revd Harding, is a living symbol of the lines from the *Magnificat*: 'He hath put down the mighty from their seat: and hath exalted the humble and meek.'

NEIL

Reverend Michael has been a very good friend of mine for many years. He is a marvellous minister.

In 2013, the university awarded me its highest degree. It was marvellous to be given an honorary degree by Keele University, which is the best university in the world.

The university has looked after me and I've looked after the university. I've known all the vice chancellors since Harold Taylor and the present one, Professor Nick Foskett, is one of the best. I don't think I would have got the degree if he hadn't become vice chancellor. I am sorry he is retiring in 2015, but I am looking forward to working with Trevor McMillan, who is taking over. He is a very nice man.

MALCOLM

In recent years, a number of us had proposed to the university that Neil should be awarded an honorary degree. A lot of people get honorary degrees when they have contributed a lot less to the university than Neil. But we never got anywhere, and I wasn't particularly optimistic. I thought universities simply don't give honorary degrees to people like Neil.

But I underestimated Keele, because, one day in the late autumn of 2012, Neil rang me to tell me that the Vice Chancellor wanted to see him. 'What do you think he wants?' I had no idea.

No sooner had Neil had his meeting with Professor Foskett than he was back on the blower with the exciting news that it was indeed about an honorary degree. He could hardly contain himself, but told me that he had been told not to tell anyone, so I had to keep it secret.

Not long after, someone else told me in confidence that Neil had been told in confidence that he was getting the degree. Then someone else told me, again in strict confidence. This happened several times over the following weeks. It became one of those secrets that everybody knows. Professor Foskett said later that Neil's degree was the worst-kept secret in the history of honorary degrees at Keele. But nobody really minded, as everyone was delighted for him.

So, on a warm summer's day in July 2013, Neil joined the graduating undergraduates and postgraduates and their parents at a ceremony in the University Chapel, at which Professor Foskett conferred an honorary master's degree on him.

Professor Foskett describes an honorary degree as the highest degree the university can award:

> Recipients of honorary degrees have had to make a distinguished contribution to the local community in some way. It is a bit like the honours list. Neil met that measure. The award of the degree illustrates the key character of Keele: warm, welcoming, open

to a diverse community and having a real sense of community spirit. Neil epitomises that.

He told a story that reminded me of what had happened to one of his predecessors, Professor David Harrison, many years before:

> When I was appointed as vice chancellor the very first written communication I had was a letter from Neil congratulating me on my appointment and inviting me to join him in the chapel. I was quite touched.
>
> Neil is very engaging and captures what Keele is all about. He always has a cheerful word to say and exudes genuine warmth. How much he means to the Keele community is recognised in his honorary degree. He has had a longer engagement with Keele than almost anyone else here, certainly longer than anyone on the staff.
>
> A lot of Keele people take him under their wing and keep a watchful eye on him. It is a slightly quirky tradition, which represents a genuine sense of social obligation. It is part of the commitment to Keele that we are all trustees for Neil, but equally he makes a very positive contribution to this community. He is part of the folklore of Keele.

The official university citation for the degree reads:

> In recognition of his life-long personal

commitment to advancing the sporting, social and charitable life of students at Keele University and in the wider community of North Staffordshire.

Neil Baldwin has been adopted by the student body over the last 54 years as something of a mascot for Keele. He has watched, supported and kept in touch with successive cohorts of Keele students building an impressive network of alumni contacts both nationally and internationally. A proud royal enthusiast and representative of Keele, Neil has even managed to collar the Duke of Edinburgh to offer his opinion on various world issues.

The Neil Baldwin Football Club features prominently in local press as Neil, who manages the club, recruits predominantly from Keele. Alongside his involvement with the chapel, Neil has been actively involved in charity fundraising through the rag. Recently Neil has focused his fundraising efforts on the Cheetham's children's ward at the University Hospital of North Staffordshire.

He serves the students offering advice and support to students, remaining steadfastly proud and loyal to Keele. In doing so he has openly defended Keele and voiced his concern about any issue that affects Keele to his numerous contacts within Parliament, the various leaders of Christian denomination churches, volunteer organizations and business leaders across the country whom he regularly visits.

Visiting alumni are often greeted by Neil and

he is instantly recognisable, even to Keele alumni from as far back as the 1960s. Neil Baldwin has remained a loyal friend of Keele and has positively contributed to the University experience of hundreds of students.

Reverend Michael Harding likes the idea that a university, whose aim is the pursuit of truth, should honour a man who speaks the truth uninhibitedly. 'Little children can come out with things you'd rather not talk about. Neil's like that. Neil will not only talk about the elephant in the room, but pat its trunk. He has a child-like (not childish) simplicity.'

The proposal to award the degree to Neil on this occasion had come from the Students' Union, and it was one of my successors as president of the union, Joe Turner, who gave the oration to present Neil with his honorary degree at the degree ceremony. He said:

> Neil Baldwin has been part of Keele for over fifty years now. He has seen every building go up around Keele except for Keele Hall (he told me he's not that old). In that time, his loyalty, openness and enthusiasm has meant that he has been adopted by the student body as a mascot for Keele.
>
> As Francis Beckett from *The Guardian* put it, 'He walked into the Students' Union in 1960, an engaging schoolboy with learning difficulties from the local town of Newcastle-under-Lyme, and became a fixture.' Nearest to Neil's heart have been the students and the Church.

Indeed, in March 1960, as a fourteen-year-old lad, Neil visited Keele campus, where his mother worked. The first places he saw were the chapel and Students' Union Nissen huts. Back then, there were few cars, no mobile phones and a limited bus service. Thoroughly enjoying his day out, Neil missed the last bus and found himself stuck on campus. Having met Neil earlier, a few students offered to put him up for the night in their hut. Speaking to Neil before today, he remembers the dinner of pie and chips with peas which they made for him.

This was the beginning of a symbiotic relationship between Neil and the students of Keele, which has continued to this day. A welcoming face from your first day starting at Keele, he has watched, supported and kept in touch with successive cohorts of Keele students, building an impressive network of alumni contacts both national and international. In return, whenever Neil is on campus there will usually be a student by his side having a chat or simply making sure he doesn't need anything.

A big part of Neil's life has been the jobs he has held in the circus as Nello the Clown, bringing joy to hundreds if not thousands of children. Neil may even be the first clown to receive an honorary degree.

He then went on to become kit man for Stoke City Football Club. Lou Macari, a former Stoke

City manager, is quoted calling Neil his 'best-ever signing' and goes on to say that, 'His real value was in helping the players relax before games. No chemist ever produced a drug that could reduce stress levels like Nello. I'm convinced that gave us an edge in matches. Nello bonded the group.'

Neil brought this enthusiasm for fun and football back to Keele, setting up the Neil Baldwin Football Club for students of any ability wanting to play. Managed by Neil, the association is chaired by Kevin Keegan and our very own chancellor, [the environmentalist and writer] Jonathon Porritt.

He told a story by Professor Linden West about the NBFC:

Cambridge University invited Neil's team for a match and, following a lavish lunch and 6–0 up towards the end of the first half of the match, they began to suspect that they might not be playing the university's official football team. Since then, though, Neil's students have returned annually to play Cambridge for the Neil Baldwin Cup.

Neil can be modest about his abilities but, with his football club's season of no defeats in all nine games played this year, we were all sure that he had good odds on becoming Stoke City's next manager before Mark Hughes was appointed.

Being a devout Christian, Neil regularly attends chapel services, helping out where he can. Neil has taken it upon himself to personally greet every potential new chaplain, treating them to lunch. It's not surprising, then, that he has met every chaplain who has ever been at Keele and his links within the church community mean that he is on first-name terms with many of the clergy in the Church of England. Neil is affectionately referred to as the Bishop of Keele.

Alongside his involvement with the chapel, Neil has been actively involved in charity fundraising through Rag, helping to raise thousands of pounds for cancer research and Alzheimer's charities. Recently, Neil has focused his fundraising efforts on the Cheetham's children's ward at the University Hospital of North Staffordshire.

He serves the students, offering advice and support to students, remaining steadfastly proud of Keele. In doing so, he's openly defended the university, voicing his concerns about any issue that may affect Keele to his numerous contacts within Parliament, the church leaders and business leaders across the country, whom he regularly visits. Being a proud royalist and ambassador for Keele, Neil has spoken to the Duke of Edinburgh to offer him a few pointers on running the country.

Our returning alumni are often greeted by Neil and he is instantly recognisable, even to the first cohorts of Keele graduates who we call our 'golden graduates'. Neil Baldwin has remained a loyal friend of Keele and has positively contributed to the university experience of hundreds of students in his time here.

I don't doubt that Neil's parents would have been very proud of the life that Neil has led and all of his achievements leading up to this special day.

Neil, resplendent in his robes, and enjoying every minute of the ceremony while characteristically displaying no nerves at all, replied:

I was told that I shouldn't write a long speech, so I've shortened it, but it was hard because I've been here for over fifty-four years. It's a great day to be at Keele.

I can actually say that I remember this place when it was all fields. I've seen every building go up (except Keele Hall).

I've met each of our four chancellors, six vice chancellors and the many thousands of students as they've come to Keele, not forgetting all the staff.

The person who sticks out most in my mind is a young lad called Malcolm Clarke. Well, he used to be a young lad. I watched him grow from the nervous first-year student to a strong union president. In his year as president, he made me an honorary member of the Students' Union, which was something I was always grateful for.

Keele has always been a welcoming place to me and I have tried to return the kindness that everyone has shown me.

The Church has always been a big part of my

life and I've made many good friends over the years, which include the chaplains, and seventy-nine students who have gone on to become part of the clergy.

I have tried to keep in touch with these students and many others to make sure that they are getting on all right.

What I've found from talking to them is that you should try to find something that you enjoy doing and always remember that, when times get tough, work hard and things will get better. I wish you every success in life and good luck with whatever you choose to do.

I never set out to get any rewards or prizes for the work that I've done because I enjoy what I do and the people I have met.

If someone had told me, all those years ago, when I first came to Keele, that I would be receiving this honour alongside a home-grown Olympic athlete, a famous businesswoman, a knight of the realm and a lord sheriff, I would have told them to stop being silly.

It is a great privilege to be given this honorary degree by the university that I love. It is a beautiful gift to receive from the Vice Chancellor and all the university staff.

I could go on and tell you lots of interesting stories about Keele and my life but I'll stop there and say: thank you very much for this honour, and congratulations to all of you graduating today.

After the ceremony Neil proudly enjoyed having his photograph taken with the Chancellor, Jonathon Porritt, and the other dignitaries, as well as his friends. Later that week he proudly attended the dinner given by the university for the honorary graduates and others. I was also privileged to attend that dinner, and it was great to see Neil getting recognition in such distinguished company.

Neil's longstanding friend, Tony Bartlett, spoke for a lot of us: 'I was never so proud of Keele as when they gave Neil his honorary master's degree. His values have been rewarded.'

NEIL

It was a great day. In 1977 Malcolm had let me wear his PhD gown on the day of his ceremony and I was photographed with it on next to my mum. Now I had my own, and it's better than his. The very day I got the degree would have been my father's hundredth birthday. How marvellous is that! I'm sure that he and my mum were very proud to see me up there getting the degree, because I know they are watching me from up there.

MALCOLM

One of the people who helped Neil prepare for the big day was Sara Pointon, the Vice Chancellor's PA. As a relative newcomer to Keele, she has her own angle on the relationship between Neil and the university:

I came to Keele in 2008 and almost immediately I was made aware of Neil. Some people tried to block him from seeing the then Vice Chancellor, Janet Finch, or just put him off in one way or another. I remember him ringing up to invite Janet to his birthday party, which I thought was a really lovely thing for him to do, but of course the message never got through.

In 2012 Neil came to see me, in connection with the decision to award him an honorary degree. We got speaking, he asked me about my son, Vincent – I have his picture in my office – and asked if he had ever been to the circus, to which I replied, no, he hadn't. So Neil then said, 'Right, I want to take you and Vincent to the circus – on me.' I didn't really think it would happen, but he kept ringing and, eventually, Family Pointon went to the circus in May 2013, and, true to his word, it was free, except, of course, that it cost us a fortune in popcorn, sweets and cans of fizzy pop for both him and Vincent.

I worked very closely with Neil during the run-up to his degree. I wanted to make sure it was an extremely special event for him.

It's the same as it was with the alumni dinners: on the few occasions that one of the Keele administrators has tried to block Neil in some way, he's just outlasted them. It is the award of the honorary degree that gives the view of the university.

Sara added:

Neil *is* Keele, and Keele is Neil. Everyone remembers him and always fondly. I am extremely proud of Neil and also of Keele, the fact that Keele is a family and has nurtured him over the years is testament to the staff and students. Neil is a friend of the family now and anything I can do to help him is done.

Neil met my nephew, Joe Clarke, who is one of Britain's canoe slalom team, at the Sports Personality of the Year awards. Richard Callaway is Nike UK director of marketing, but is also an alumnus of Keele. Nike have recently taken Joe on as one of his sponsors and Richard is also on our council here at Keele. We got round to talking about Neil and *Marvellous*. Richard said he remembers being accommodated in Barnes Hall and Neil would come into their flat during the day, just chatting and sitting. They would eventually have to leave and go to lectures, and when they came back he would still be sitting there. But, again, this gives me a warm feeling, because where else would that have happened?

CHAPTER NINE

NEIL: THE BIOPIC

MALCOLM

In 2010 Francis Beckett and I had a late-night conversation about Neil's fiftieth-anniversary celebrations of his time at Keele, what he has achieved and what he means to Keele. The result was a *Guardian* feature on 9 March 2010, under the headline 'How Neil Baldwin became Keele University's mascot'. Francis's piece began:

> Last weekend, Keele University celebrated Neil Baldwin's 50th anniversary there. It was a splendid two-day affair, with speeches from distinguished alumni, a dinner, a testimonial football match, and a service of thanksgiving for his work conducted by the Bishop of Lichfield, a Keele graduate.
>
> But Baldwin has never worked at Keele in any

capacity, or been a student there, or had any formal connection with the place. He walked into the students' union in 1960, an engaging schoolboy with learning difficulties from the local town of Newcastle-under-Lyme, and became a fixture.

Television dramatist Peter Bowker saw the piece and thought it the perfect subject for a drama documentary. It was drawn to Peter's attention by his wife, who thought he would be interested in it – before he was a writer, Peter had worked for many years in the learning-disability field.

Peter spoke to Patrick Spence, the managing director of Fifty Fathoms Films, and Patrick, via *The Guardian* and Francis, found his way to me.

Patrick wanted to make it. He was hoping to persuade the BBC to buy it, and was quite confident that he could do so, because of Peter's reputation with the BBC.

Patrick asked me if I thought that Neil would agree to a film being made of his life, because, if he wouldn't, there would be no point in taking the idea any further. I replied that there would be many questions about such a film, but the one question I could be sure I knew the answer to was that Neil would definitely love the idea of a film being made about his life. I could vouch for that.

NEIL

I was very pleased when Malcolm told me that the BBC were thinking about making a film about my life – because it's been a great life. I couldn't wait for it to get started.

MALCOLM

I met with Patrick and Peter in London to discuss the project. My major initial concern was that I didn't want a film to be made that in any way mocked Neil. I realised, after meeting Patrick and Peter, that there was no way they would want to do that. Peter wanted to make a positive film about Neil's life and his remarkable achievements. It would be funny, and at one level that humour might be seen to be at Neil's expense, but it would present Neil's remarkable achievements in a positive light, and he would emerge triumphant. I returned to Manchester reassured.

But first they had to sell the idea to the BBC. It was more than two years before we learned that BBC2 had commissioned it and it was all systems go. Neil was impatient for news. 'Have you heard any more about the film?' would be his weekly question outside Britannia Stadium, and on the phone between games. 'No, Neil, I haven't. I'll let you know as soon as I do.'

We agreed that the next step would be for me to introduce Peter and Patrick to Neil at Keele. The captain of the Neil Baldwin Football Club turned up at the meeting. Neil said, 'Do you mind if Angad, my captain, is here?' 'Not at all,' I said, but I was mildly surprised that he had come. After about twenty minutes, Angad made his apologies and left.

I then realised that he had probably come just to check us out. When Neil had told him that he was meeting some people who were making a film about his life, he probably thought that this was an unlikely event, although anybody who knows Neil well should, of course, learn to be cautious about making such an assumption. I think he wanted to make sure that this was not some sort of a scam and that Neil was not being exploited. I felt that this perfectly summed up Neil's relationship with Keele students. For over half a century there has been a real sense in which he has looked after them, but they have also looked after him.

NEIL

I don't know why it took a long time for the film to be made. This was very frustrating. I think Malcolm got fed up of me always asking him when we were going to hear something.

Anyway, when it started, Malcolm brought Patrick and Peter along and introduced them. Peter is a great writer and he was pleased to have the chance to write about my great life. Patrick is a very nice man, and asked me if I was happy to have the film made. I said, of course I am. My life will make a great film.

A bit later, Peter brought the director, Julian Farino and Toby Jones, who was to play me, up from London. We sat in a private room in Keele Hall and they started to discuss the project with me.

I liked Toby and I was very pleased that he was playing me, even though he is not quite as good-looking as I am. He's a great actor, one of the best. He did a great job. I originally thought the part ought to go to Rowan Atkinson, and that's who I recommended when they asked me who should play me, but I think Toby was a lot better than he would have been.

MALCOLM

I was fascinated by the conversation. Julian, as the director, was very interested in how events came to happen, what caused them and how they were linked to each other, and Neil's relationships with the people in his life.

Toby was clearly trying to get inside Neil's head, to understand what makes him tick, what makes him happy, what makes him angry and what makes him sad. Because of Neil's unfailing positivity, this proved to be something of a challenge and at times I could feel Toby struggling to get underneath Neil's contented exterior. What he probably didn't fully appreciate at the time was that this is actually who the real Neil is.

At one point he asked Neil a question that slightly took me aback because I had never asked it myself or heard anybody else ask him before: had he ever had a girlfriend? Neil replied that he had one once, many years ago, when he was working at the pottery, but it hadn't come to anything. And that's where it was left.

I felt that Julian and Toby were understandably a little nervous about meeting Neil for the first time. I am not an actor, but I could see that, if you are playing a living character, you would be concerned that they like you and are happy with you. That would be true for any living character, but probably more so when you are playing someone as unusual as Neil. Also, while playing Neil was an exciting and colourful undertaking, it was a role that could also present considerable challenges.

Tiger Aspect filmed at Neil's honorary-degree ceremony. Over tea afterwards, I was talking to Patrick and the Vice

Chancellor, Professor Nick Foskett. Patrick was explaining the budgetary constraints that might apply to making a film like this and at one point indicated that it might be necessary to film the university scenes at a college in London. The Vice Chancellor replied, with an appropriate degree of slightly understated firmness, 'We would be very disappointed if it wasn't filmed at Keele.'

Good for you, I thought. I too would have been very disappointed if it had not been filmed at Keele, as most certainly would Neil. Patrick reached the same view, and it was.

Peter undertook extensive research in writing the script. He spent a lot of time with Neil's friends, including me and Vic Trigg, as well as, of course, Lou Macari, members of Mary's Christadelphian Church, and others.

The result was an outstanding script, which has recently been recognised by the Best Writer award at the Royal Television Society. Iain McCullum, Tiger Aspect's head of publicity, says:

> I first read Peter's script *en route* from Glasgow to London on a packed train in January 2014. I have read many hundreds of scripts over the course of my career as a publicist but none affected me quite so deeply as this one did. Peter's wonderful narrative resonated from its first beat. I was carried along from scene to scene, never daring to put it down. And then I burst into tears. A lady opposite me asked what was the matter. I said I had been reading a wonderful story and felt

already that I knew the characters and wanted to know them more.

I knew that *Marvellous* would be a hit from Page One and texted Patrick Spence to say as much. Our *Marvellous* journey continued and over the course of the next ten months I became part of a wonderful cast and crew, led by brilliant producer Katie Swinden, all of whom embraced this project with open hearts and great creativity. I watched Toby Jones work with Julian Farino and saw the magic they were creating.

And of course I met Neil Baldwin and also got to know those close to him for many years. Their devotion to Neil further reassured me that this story had to be told and when it was I was delighted to learn that *Marvellous* had the same affect on millions of others as it had on me on that train journey.

Tiger Aspect decided to set up their filming HQ in an office in Keele village, with almost all the filming done at the university and in North Staffordshire. The furthest they went afield were the football grounds at Crewe Alexander FC and Wrexham FC. Once the show was on the road, it was very intense. Filming took place throughout May 2014 at various locations.

Katie Swinden, the producer, said to Neil when we met her for the first time in the North Staffs hotel, 'You must come and join us on the set for one or two days, Neil.' Neil replied instantly, 'I'll be there every day,' which was a statement, not a request. And so it proved. He was there every day, keeping an eye on the proceedings.

NEIL

It was great that it was all filmed locally. Before it started I sat in the office in Keele village stencilling some of the signs used in the film. They gave me plenty of tea and biscuits and I made them all laugh with my jokes.

I watched nearly all the filming. I had my own director's chair and my own private dressing room with 'Real Neil' on the door, next to Toby and all the other actors. I really enjoyed having my meals in the catering trucks with all the actors and crew. They were very good meals.

MALCOLM

Toby DeCann, a Stoke City season-ticket holder, who played Paddy in the film, says:

> When my agent called me I don't think I had ever heard so much excitement in his voice. 'They're looking for [actors to play] Stoke City players for a film about a kit man. This has you written all over it.' Like most people I was amazed to discover that the BBC were going to shoot a film in Staffordshire, but I was even more surprised to find out that the subject was going to be Neil 'Nello' Baldwin. Neil was a stalwart of Lou Macari's red-and-white army in the early nineties and was just as notable and legendary as some of the players of my boyhood club in that era.

When I read the early draft of Peter Bowker's fantastic script it truly brought a tear to my eye. It captured not only the essence of Neil as a human being but also the values of the football club and the spirit of the city of Stoke-on-Trent. It's the people of the Potteries that make the area what it is: a friendly, warm and welcoming place with family at its heart – and Neil is one of its favourite sons. It was then that I realised I had to be involved with this production.

Fortunately, on the eve of my audition, I was able to get in touch with the former Stoke defender Lee Sandford, who was so generous with his time. He recounted dozens of tales about dressing-room banter, pitch-side pranks and away-day shenanigans involving the players, Lou and Nello. He said, 'I remember regularly being in tears and doubled over with the constant laughter that Nello brought to the team.'

So, with plenty of determination, a nineties Stoke shirt and a few stories in my pocket, I headed to London the next day to audition for *Marvellous*. It was here that I met the director, Julian Farino, who approached me in the waiting room and commented on my football top. 'Where did you get that?' he asked. His face lit up when I explained that it was a hand-me-down from my dad.

Now, as an actor, when your audition for a role in a film lasts forty-five minutes, you get the impression that you've made an impression. We talked about Stoke City, Crystal Palace (Julian is a fanatical supporter), Tony Pulis [a former Stoke manager], 'Delilah' [a song featured in the film], oatcakes and of course, Neil Baldwin. When we finally got to reading the script, Julian smiled at me and said, 'I hope this is going to be good.'

Julian is meticulous as a director but is also a great leader and motivator of a team. His catchphrase 'We can do this!' is one that lives long in my memory from working on *Marvellous*, and is one that I pinch off him and use from time to time. He's the best director I've ever worked with.

So, after a few weeks of waiting, I was delighted when my agent called to tell me that I would be playing the part of Stoke player Paddy in the film. About a week later I visited the set at Keele University to do a costume test and, the night before, the producer, Katie Swinden, phoned me with a strange request.

'You're a season-ticket holder at Stoke, aren't you Toby?' she quizzed. 'Would you be willing to stand in front of the Boothen End at this weekend's game against Fulham and get the crowd going with some "There's only one Neil Baldwin" chants?'

Without hesitation I agreed. But I could hear some trepidation in her voice. It wasn't until I was on the set at Keele during a break in filming, having a quiet chat with Julian Farino and Peter Bowker, that I realised what the apprehension was. 'Will they know who he is?' asked Julian.

'They won't shout abuse and not go along with it, will they?' said Peter. I assured them that the Stoke supporters never forget and if they put Neil Baldwin on that pitch then they were sure to get one heck of a reaction.

Sure enough, just before kick-off on Saturday, 3 May 2014, a packed Boothen End stood up in unison to salute Nello. I have to admit that standing there nervously with a microphone in my hand with Neil Baldwin at my side in front of the most vociferous section of the Stoke City faithful was one of the proudest moments of my life. I think I said something cheesy like 'Good afternoon, Boothen End. Let's show a national television audience how we do it in Stoke-on-Trent. Let's do it for Nello!'

The roar was deafening as the crowd joined in as I led with the 'There's only one Neil Baldwin!' and 'Nello! Nello!' chants. Julian, Peter and Katie were absolutely delighted that they were able to get the footage, which became the bookend to the film. They thanked me hugely, but for me it was the fans that deserved all the credit. They were the ones who turned up early in their seats to show their appreciation for Nello. It was definitely a turning point in the production and there was no question that the Stoke City family was on board with *Marvellous*.

The shooting of the film was an absolute dream. Many highlights stick out for me, such as standing in the tunnel and running out onto the pitch at Wrexham (which doubled as the Victoria Ground), working with the genius that is Toby Jones and witnessing the remarkable performance of Tony Curran – who I still call 'Boss' – as Lou Macari. From day one *Marvellous* felt like a team effort and everyone, from the talent to the production team to the catering staff, was passionate about telling Neil's story, which turned out to be one of the best television dramas of 2014.

Sometimes during a production magic happens and you can't quite put your finger on why it's occurring. I think maybe it was Neil's positive outlook and fifty years in show business that rubbed off on everyone. I congratulate you, sir, for the well-deserved recognition that *Marvellous* has brought you and thank you for being an honest and true friend.

NEIL

The first time all the actors came together was at the first read-through. This was held in the Putney Boat Club building next to the River Thames. I love Putney and it was strange that it was held there, because I've been there many times for the Boat Race. Malcolm and Vic came along, too. I showed them all the Boat Race places.

MALCOLM

Before the read-through started, I was chatting with Gemma Jones, who was playing Mary. Gemma said she was tired, as she had just flown in from New York, and would I mind if she sat down, so I thought that the read-through might have to be rather a mechanical process for her. How wrong could you be? As soon as it started, Gemma came alive. Afterwards, I told her that it felt quite spooky as I almost felt that Mary was back with us in the room. I thought all the actors in the film were brilliant, but for me Gemma's performance as Mary was a standout. Of course, unlike the position for the other characters, neither Peter, the writer, nor Gemma could speak to the real Mary, which made her portrayal even more remarkable.

NEIL

The read-through was great. It was the first time I had heard the whole film. I found out afterwards that Patrick was watching me closely to see if I got upset with some bits, such as when my mum died, because they didn't want me to be upset. That was very nice of him, but I was OK. Mum wouldn't want me to be upset, and I know she's watching me. Some of the others weren't OK. There were some hankies out and the sound of sniffing in the room.

MALCOLM

I also watched a lot of the filming which was a fascinating and for me completely new experience. Filming was to a tight schedule and so it meant that everything had to operate like clockwork. Simon, the assistant director, made sure that the whole operation kept moving at as fast a pace as possible, always dependent on the number of times Julian, the director, wanted to reshoot a particular scene. I was greatly impressed with the professionalism, teamwork and kindness of the whole crew. Despite the pressure they were working under, nothing seemed to be too much trouble for them in looking after Neil or his visitors.

Neil sat in his chair supervising the proceedings, giving the thumbs-up to Toby Jones and the others after each take, and being kept fed and watered by the support crew.

Scenes were shot repeatedly, up to a dozen times in some cases, until Julian was quite satisfied with the output. Even then, the scene might have to be reshot while the cameras focused on a different actor or a different perspective.

One of the extras, who was also working as an extra on the daytime TV series *Doctors*, told me that on *Doctors* the second or third take usually had to do, because they didn't have the time for multiple takes; but on this filming there would seemingly be as many takes as needed to get to the standard that Julian required.

I commented to Greg McHugh that it was strange to see somebody playing me, and he replied that it was strange for him because he had never played a character with the real-life person standing at the side watching him. He said that, if I didn't like the way he was playing me, I should speak to Julian, because he has to play it the way the director instructs. But I was more than happy. My wife, Lesley, remarked to him that it had been very good married to him all these years.

There are things you never realise until you watch a film being made. For example, *Marvellous* includes a lot of scenes of people eating, usually Neil. Toby Jones clearly could not eat a dozen chocolate biscuits if a scene had to be shot twelve

Neil Baldwin F.C.

Neil Baldwin
Testimonial Match

Kick Off - 2.00pm
Keele University

Official Programme
60p

Sunday March 12th 2000

President Kevin Keegan (England Coach)
Player Manager - Neil Baldwin

NBAFC V's ALL STARS XI

Referee - Mr U. D Rennie - Sheffield

Above left: NBFC away at Rocester in 2014. Brad is in the back row, third from right.

Above right: The match programme from Neil's testimonial match in March 2000. Kevin Keegan's letter to Neil was printed inside.

Below: Another unstoppable penalty from the inspirational player-manager.

Left: Gordon Banks leads out his All-Stars team at Newcastle Town for the game against NBFC.

Right: Famous footballers Joey Barton, Robbie Fowler, David James and Steve McManaman join Neil on an official NBFC Christmas card.

A VERY MERRY CHRISTMAS FROM N.B.A.F.C.

Below: Neil greets England and Stoke City legend Peter Shilton in his Derby County days.

Left: Winnie and footballer Simon Sturridge give Neil his leaving present on the pitch at the Britannia Stadium.

Below: Captain Neil with referee Uriah Rennie, officials and opposing captain Chic Bates.

Above: Neil and Uriah at the post-match presentation with Chic Bates looking on.

Above: Neil and the Bishop in the procession in Keele chapel for Neil's forty years' thanksgiving service. Malcolm is in shot bottom left.

Below: The Bishop of Leeds adds his signature to Neil's Bible in 2015.

Left: Malcolm applauds Neil and Mike Sheron on the naming of 'Baldwin's Bar'.

Right: Malcolm compères 'This Is Your Life Neil Baldwin' for a modest Neil.

Left: John Easom makes a telling contribution at a celebration for Neil, with Malcolm looking on.

St PAUL'S
CATHEDRAL

Eucharist

with the Ordination and Consecration of

The Reverend Canon Tim Dakin

General Secretary of the Church Missionary Society,
and of the South American Missionary Society,
Canon Theologian of Coventry Cathedral,
as Bishop of Winchester

and

The Venerable John Wraw

the Archdeacon of Wiltshire,
to be Bishop of Bradwell in the Diocese of Chelmsford

Feast of the Conversion of Paul

Wednesday 25th January 2012
11 am

Above left: Neil's order of service, signed by innumerable bishops, all of whom are 'very good friends'.

Above right: Peter Coates, Stoke City FC Chairman, joins Neil in endorsing local Labour candidate Tristram Hunt in the 2015 General Election.

Below: Neil, Malcolm and Lesley celebrating on Neil's honorary degree day.

Left: A proud day for Neil as Professor Nick Foskett, Keele Vice-Chancellor, awards Neil his honorary degree.

Right: Neil sings a duet with Beatie Wolfe at Hayfield.

Left: *Midlands Today* film part of the 'Neil Baldwin choir' from *Marvellous* in Fenton Community Centre, Stoke.

Above: Neil shares a joke with Peter Bowker during the filming of *Marvellous*.

Below left: Neil prepares the flock of sheep which, as a Freeman of Stoke-on-Trent, he is now entitled to drive through the city.

Below right: Neil addresses the BAFTA audience with Peter Bowker, Toby Jones and Gemma Jones looking on.

times. Therefore, at the end of each such scene, someone rushed on with a bucket and a tissue to allow Toby to disgorge the food from his mouth without his having swallowed it.

I loved the way that, once Toby was made up as Neil, he didn't like to come out of character. On one occasion he was in a scene with a couple of extras that was being filmed when I arrived. Between takes, I gave a small wave of recognition. He beckoned to the two extras to come over and have a word with me and said in his Neil voice, 'I'd like to introduce you to Malcolm Clarke. He's the chairman of the Football Supporters' Federation and a member of the FA Council; he's a very good friend of mine.'

NEIL

I appeared myself in a few scenes. One day they were filming a scene with me and Toby and at the end of the take Julian said, 'Neil, that was absolutely great, but, Toby, I'm afraid we will have to take it again.' So I was a better actor than he was. I like telling people that story.

MALCOLM

I had not realised that there is such a job as a football choreographer, who is paid to instruct actors playing a football match on how to make it look realistic. It was interesting to see the recreation of the match refereed by Uriah Rennie, which Zara and I had watched at Keele all those years earlier, refereed in the film by Uriah himself. Uriah and I were able to advise on what had happened. The scene where Neil comes on to play for Stoke included a number of regular Stoke City supporters.

It was very interesting talking to some of the extras who formed the crowd in the recreation of the testimonial at Wrexham FC. I was surprised to discover that they didn't really know much, if anything, of what the film was about. Apparently, this is normal for extras, who turn up to do particular scenes and often aren't told. And, indeed, many didn't appear to be bothered about what the film was about or where their particular scene fitted in.

The only scene I saw filmed that didn't require multiple retakes was, paradoxically, the one for which you might have expected the most retakes: when Toby is required to head the ball for Neil's 'goal' during the game. Toby stood on a stool, with the chief cameraman, David Odd, flat on his back underneath him to film it from below. Someone then threw the ball into the air and Toby had to jump off the stool and head it. Immediately before the first take Toby said, 'This is where I make a complete fool of myself.' And I'm sure most of us expected that this scene would require multiple retakes. In fact, on the first occasion the ball was lobbed in the air, Toby jumped from the stool and met it perfectly with his forehead. To our astonishment, Julian said that was fine, no need for any more takes.

On one occasion, prior to the filming of a scene involving 'real' Lou and the 'film' Lou, Lou said to Tony Curran, who was playing him, 'Have you any advice on how to say my lines?'

Tony replied, 'Lou, I'm playing you – you should be telling me how to say the lines!'

NEIL

They did the scene of my mum's funeral in the same Christadelphian Church in Dimsdale Parade, Newcastle, where the real funeral was held eleven years earlier. Some of the extras who provided the congregation for that scene were members of the Christadelphian Church who had been at the real funeral, including Les Bailey, who took Mum's funeral, and his wife Mary.

Malcolm was crying in the funeral scene but I told him there was no need to. I cried when Mum died but she wouldn't want me to be still crying now. You just have to get on with life and make the most of it. In any case, I know she's watching me.

MALCOLM

Les Bailey recalls:

> We weren't expecting to see the coffin in the church, which quite shocked us when we walked in, but, on thinking about it, we realised that, of course, it had to be there. The church members also found it odd to be asked by the director to put on particular facial expressions.

In fact, it was a bit surreal for all of us – like going to someone's funeral twice. We were watching on a monitor in a side room. I was sitting next to Neil. When Toby began Neil's oration, which was very similar to the oration he had given at the real funeral, I found it so moving that I could not hold it together. A member of the production crew discreetly stepped forward with some tissues to help me out and whispered in my ear, 'She's in a better place now.' This was sensitive and thoughtful, intended to make me feel better; but, in fact, it made me think, this is ridiculous, there isn't anyone in that coffin. Neil, who was sitting next to me, wasn't crying and said in his characteristic, straightforward way, 'What are you crying for? There's no need to cry. It was eleven years ago. She's up there watching us, and she'll be very pleased. Will you get me a cup of tea?' Back to reality.

At the end of the funeral scene, Julian's direction required that the only guest still eating the buffet at the end of the funeral scene was me. My family say Julian did that after watching me scoff the catering on set, but I am convinced that it was just a coincidence.

Outside afterwards I told Toby about my tears and he said thank you and gave me a hug, which wasn't the response I had expected. I suddenly realised that, if you tell an actor that he's made you cry, it's a big professional compliment.

While they were shooting the scene in the hospital corridor at the City General Hospital, in the middle of a take the real Neil unexpectedly appeared out of a side corridor in a wheelchair being pushed by a real member of the hospital staff right through the middle of the set. Neil just said calmly, 'She's taking me to see the hospital chapel.' Apparently he was oblivious of the fact that he had just interrupted filming, and half the crew were shaking with laughter.

Neil's old friend, teacher Tony Bartlett, used the filming as part of his curriculum.

I took some of the lads that I teach down to watch some of the filming of *Marvellous* in the Iron Market in Newcastle. They all said, 'Can't we see the real Neil?' And they said the best thing about the whole day was meeting the real Neil. He had that effect on them much more than Toby Jones or Katie the producer.

The filming saw Neil's only known failure to get an invitation. He found out somehow that Toby Jones was getting married later in the year, and, naturally, he said, 'Can I come to your wedding, Toby?' Toby thought about it, then he said, quite nicely, 'No, Neil, you can't.' Neil told me Toby was joking, but I felt fairly sure he wasn't. The story got around the film crew, and I'm afraid they rather enjoyed embarrassing Toby with it. At the post-production party they started singing, to the tune of 'Guantanamera', 'Come to your wed-ding, / He's gonna come to your wed-ding...'

NEIL

It was a great night, that post-production party. It was in the Glebe pub in Stoke and all the actors were there, and they sang the song 'Delilah' from the film, and they gave me a book, which they'd all signed for me. It was a really great night.

I was invited to a small private showing of the film in advance of its premiere, along with Malcolm and Vic. I think Peter, Patrick and Katie were a little nervous about what we'd think, especially what *I'd* think. But we thought it was great. So did the TV critics, and so did the audiences at the two premieres, in London and Stoke-on-Trent.

These premieres were great. I appeared on stage and took questions. It was shown on BBC2 on 25 September 2014, and repeated on Christmas Day, and it's won lots of awards.

I keep in touch with some of the actors too. Nick Gleaves, who played Rev. Mark, rings me up quite often and we have a good talk. Rev. Mark was a character Pete Bowker invented. He put most of the vicars in my life into one character.

Malcolm and I watched the TV broadcast of the film on 25 September at a showing organised by the Students' Union in the ballroom of the union building. It seemed the most appropriate place. I've been at Keele and in the union all those years.

It was marvellous to watch *Marvellous* in the Students' Union with a lot of students who I knew. Everybody thought it was great. The BBC did interviews with me and with and a number of students who have played for my football team and know me from Keele.

MALCOLM

At the end of the film, Neil was called upon to say a few words and answer some questions. He said to me, 'Will you introduce me?' Of course, but it wasn't easy to sum up Neil's fifty years at Keele and our friendship in a few minutes.

It was quite strange but entirely appropriate to be doing that in the Students' Union ballroom, forty-six years after I had spoken in the same room against taking direct action and occupying the registry and had proposed Neil's honorary union membership.

The BBC were filming for their *Inside Out* programme, which had an excellent feature on Neil. Earlier in the day I had been interviewed by them. Two senior Keele officials, Chris Stone, the press officer, and John Easom, the alumni manager, were there. I offered to 'brand up' (to use the marketing jargon) with the new Keele tie if one could be provided. Chris and John were very keen on this, but their efforts on their mobiles to get one brought to me didn't succeed. They may not have had the clout to rustle up a tie at short notice, but, fortunately, we had someone with us who did.

NEIL
I saw someone I knew who works near the vice chancellor's office walking by and said, 'Louise, tell Sara that Malcolm wants a university tie.' Sara is the vice chancellor's assistant. A few minutes later, Sara turned up with the tie and Malcolm put it on.

MALCOLM
Uriah Rennie told me:

> I was very pleased to appear in *Marvellous* as myself. It's not always the good and the great who should have their life catalogued. That's why this film is so important.
>
> I'm a patron of Disability Sport England and teenage cancer charities. People who are connected with those organisations have come up to me and said how inspirational they found the story as

portrayed in the film to be. They've said to me, 'It must have been one of the best things that you've been involved in.'

I was at a Bury-versus-Exeter City game, when Steve Perryman, who was a famous player for Spurs, came up to me and had a chat about the film. He told me that he had told the club's apprentice footballers, 'You must watch it, because it has so much to tell you about determination, achieving your goals and an attitude to life.' He's thinking about inviting Neil down to give a pre-season talk on motivation and positivity.

CHAPTER TEN

NEIL BALDWIN, CELEBRITY

NEIL

After the London premiere of *Marvellous* came the Stoke one. Everyone was there: councillors, people from Keele, Stoke City, Lou Macari, Malcolm and his family. It was a great night, and I was very happy to see so many people there. I enjoyed going onto the stage to say a few words. It was introduced by the northern director of the BBC, and hosted by Perry Spillar of Radio Stoke. Perry is a very good friend of mine. I knew his father many years ago, when he was a curate in Clayton, Newcastle-under-Lyme. I know he was nervous but he did very well.

MALCOLM

Neil's right. Perry Spillar *was* nervous:

I came up to North Staffordshire about six years ago, initially to Signal Radio, and about two years ago I joined Radio Stoke. About three years ago I was in the pantomime, playing the Emperor. Neil is a big fan of pantomime, and we met outside the theatre door.

It was then that I realised he was the same person that I'd seen as a teenager in Stratford all those years ago.

Although I'd never lived here until six years ago, and was born after my parents had moved away from the area, Neil provides a connection to my parents' time here.

The Stoke premiere was a quite important gig for me because there were important people from the BBC there. Neil, on the other hand, was completely unfazed by it. He even took the mike from me at one point and almost took the event over. He's no respecter of rank and treats everyone the same, even though he's a 'collector' of the great and the good. The bunfight after the premiere was very animated and very positive. It has had a good effect on the area.

The producer thinks we've had him on Radio Stoke about ten times in connection with the film. Neil's something unique. It's about attitudes to people with learning difficulties and how we should never write people off. Neil plays to his strengths. The Radio Stoke listeners love him. Our audience profile tends to be people from their mid-forties onwards. They've all heard of him. And he means a great deal to Stoke.

NEIL

At the party afterwards I sang a solo of 'How Great Thou Art'. I was also invited to go onto the pitch before the next Stoke City home game against Newcastle United.

MALCOLM

That was followed by a much bigger but marvellous fuss at the following home game against Swansea, which Stoke City designated a *'Marvellous* matchday'. The match programme featured Neil and the film, and there was clown face-painting for the kids. In a nice gesture by the club, the full choir from the film were invited as guests and came onto the pitch at half-time, along with Neil himself, resplendent in his tuxedo, who was interviewed.

We were there with Neil, writer Peter Bowker, Greg McHugh, who played me, and Toby DeCann. The man in the tuxedo held the show.

There was a magical moment in our box when Peter was talking about Gordon Banks. Neil asked the staff member looking after us to 'go and get Gordon. Peter would like to meet him.' Peter didn't take this seriously but the look on his face when, ten minutes later, there was a knock on the door and in walked arguably the world's greatest ever goalkeeper, was priceless. Neil introduced them to each other.

NEIL

Of course, I have known Gordon very well ever since the 1970s. He's a very good friend of mine. And I'm delighted that we were both given the Freedom of the City on the same day. It was 16 October 2014 when two councillors proposed it, Andrew Munday and Paul Breeze, who sadly didn't live to see it bestowed on me. I went to his funeral. He was a good man.

MALCOLM

After the Swansea game, Nicolle Begović, the wife of the Stoke goalkeeper Asmir Begović, tweeted that she wanted to meet Nello. Kath Shawcross, the wife of the Stoke City captain Ryan Shawcross, tweeted back that he could be found outside the ticket office after each game. After the next game she came out with her husband to live her dream and meet Neil. They then offered Neil a lift home, but there was a hitch.

NEIL

Malcolm had set off to the car park to fetch his car up to the ground to give me a lift, and my bag was in his boot, so I couldn't accept Asmir and Nicolle's offer, which was a shame for her.

MALCOLM

Some Banksy-type graffiti appeared overnight on the wall of a newsagent's shop in the middle of Stoke. It depicted the Queen 'knighting' with a sword the kneeling figure of a yellow chicken, with the caption 'Arise Sir Nello'.

This followed the starting of a 'Give Nello a knighthood' Facebook page.

NEIL

Since the film came out, I have been very busy. I opened a painting shop in the Potteries Shopping Centre. I was asked to switch on four sets of Christmas lights: in Meir, Stoke town centre, Bentilee and of course the Christmas tree outside the Students' Union at Keele, which I switch on every year.

That meant I couldn't go down to London and present one of the football awards for the Football Supporters' Federation, which Malcolm is chair of. They wanted me to come, with Toby Jones if he was free, and show some clips from the film. It would have been good. But it was the same day I was due to turn the Christmas tree lights on for the Students' Union at Keele, and I always do that, every year. I couldn't let them down.

In March the next year I had to turn down something else I'd have liked to go to: the Royal Television Society Awards in London. I had been invited to go to the dinner and awards ceremony, which I would have loved to do, but I had already promised to go to an event at St Hilary's Church in Wallasey, where Auntie Iris got married and where I used to go as a child with my mum when we were staying at Auntie Iris's. I couldn't let my cousin and everybody there down.

I met the Tuesday Fellowship, a club for the older parishioners, which meets in the afternoon. We had a lovely lunch of home-made soup, and then they showed clips from the film, followed by a question-and-answer session with me and Malcolm. Malcolm and I work together as a team. Vic gave me a lift there and back. It was really good to see my auntie's old friend Betty Cartwright, who reminded me of the time Canon Maurice Marshall made the mistake of thinking I was a vicar.

You can see a video of it on the Chester Diocesan website (at http://www.chester.anglican.org/news.asp?Page=821#. VYGw4_lViko). I told them that I always wanted to be ordained but it never happened. But many vicars have told me that I don't need to be ordained to do my ministry. I reminded them that Christ died on the cross for us.

I sang a solo of 'Abba Father' with the vicar, Rev. Andrew Greenhough, accompanying me on the guitar. I'm a good singer. Andrew said that his wife had been a student at Keele in the 1980s and remembered me. The parishioners seemed to really enjoy the afternoon.

Afterwards we were invited for tea by the Bishop of Birkenhead. He had some lovely cakes and he is a very nice man. He invited me back to take part in their mission work, which I will.

It was marvellous to learn afterwards that Peter Bowker had won a Writers' Guild of Great Britain Award in London. He deserved that.

MALCOLM

As always, Neil had no nerves on these occasions. Despite his newfound fame and the celebrity events, both of which he enjoys, once he has made a commitment, he will not backtrack on it or forget his commitment to his family, or the places or events that have been a central part of his life. His values are the same as they've always been, and so are his loyalties. At his heart, he's a man of strong loyalties and great integrity.

NEIL

Four days after the film was first broadcast, it was the *real* Fresher's Mart at Keele University at the start of the new academic year. It was very similar to the scene shown in the film, with me having my stall for my football club and trying to sign up students. The Students' Union was packed out.

I signed 128 players up for NBFC that day, including quite a few girls, so we might even start a women's team. I rang Malcolm in the evening to give him the good news.

I was interviewed by the *Daily Mail* and *The Independent* for feature articles about my life.

MALCOLM

The day the *Daily Mail* journalist came to Keele happened also to be the day of a visit by Dr Rowan Williams, the former Archbishop of Canterbury. During the afternoon Rowan Williams was doing a question-and-answer session with members of the Christian community at Keele in the University Chapel. I told the reporter that Neil was in the chapel with Rowan Williams; she looked a little sceptical. Sara, the vice chancellor's assistant, who is a good friend of Neil's, went across to extract Neil from the Williams meeting.

At the end of Neil's interview with the *Daily Mail*, we went to take some photographs outside the chapel. In the middle of this Rowan Williams emerged and, as he walked by, he gave Neil a cheery wave. If she had been in any doubt before, the *Daily Mail* reporter now knew for certain that Rowan Williams is a very good friend of Neil's.

NEIL

I have known quite a few of the Archbishops of Canterbury. I told Rowan Williams that he was one of the best.

MALCOLM

In the early evening Rowan Williams was giving a lecture entitled 'Mysticism and Spirituality – Two Worlds or One?' There was nothing more certain than that Neil would be going and I decided that I would go along too.

After the lecture the Friends of Keele University were hosting a dinner for Dr Williams in Keele Hall. I asked Neil if he would like me to get us two tickets for the dinner. I knew what his answer would be.

The dinner was held in Keele Hall on circular tables of ten. When I examined the table plan I saw that the University had placed Neil and me at the same table as Rowan Williams, who had the host, Professor David Shepherd, dean of the Faculty of Humanities and Social Sciences, on his right, me on his left and Neil on *my* left. It was a nice gesture by Professor Shepherd and I knew it would lead to an entertaining evening of discussion.

NEIL

The university put Malcolm, not me, next to Dr Williams. I thought they might have put me there, not Malcolm. But it was fine because I could speak to Rowan Williams. I told Dr Williams that the former Bishop of Winchester, Michael Scott-Joynt, had died. Rowan Williams hadn't heard that. Michael Scott-Joynt was a very good friend of mine, who had been Bishop of Stafford. His birthday was the same day as mine and we sent each other birthday cards every year, as well as Christmas cards. This year his wife still sent me a birthday card. It was very nice of her to remember, even though Bishop Michael had died. He died on the same day that my film was broadcast on TV. He was a good man.

Dr Williams said that he would need to find out when the funeral was, and I promised to let him know.

MALCOLM

I suppose I shouldn't have been surprised that Neil was more up to date on such matters than the most recent Archbishop of Canterbury.

Dr Williams is now the master of Magdalen College in Cambridge University. With Neil's Cambridge connections, the conversation inevitably turned to these matters. Dr Williams said, in the way that people do on these occasions, 'If you're ever coming down to Cambridge, Neil, you must get in touch.'

What I knew, but Dr Williams didn't, was that, three weeks later, the Neil Baldwin Football Club were to spend a weekend in Cambridge, playing against Selwyn College on the Saturday and Downing College on the Sunday. Uriah Rennie had agreed to travel down from his Sheffield home to referee them both.

Neil replied, 'We're coming to Cambridge to play some

football matches in three weeks' time.' He then produced a book and a pen, which he passed to Rowan Williams and said, 'Write your phone number in there.' And, of course, Dr Williams duly did. He could hardly refuse, having made the offer just a couple of minutes before. He may not have known, but I did, that a visit from Neil was now a cast-iron certainty.

In his after-dinner speech, Dr Williams commented, 'I have been sitting next to Neil, a famous film star, and, as you can imagine, we've had a very interesting evening of discussion.' Neil intervened to say, 'I told him that he is one of the best Archbishops of Canterbury we have ever had.'

NEIL

Unfortunately, when NBFC visited Cambridge, Rowan Williams wasn't in when I rang him, but it is good to have his number for the next time we go there.

It was a great weekend. We were looked after, and we won both the games: we beat Downing College 5–2 and Selwyn College 4–3. It was great to have Uriah refereeing both games. His daughter is at Cambridge University, so being able to visit her was an added bonus for him.

Over the years I have been to Cambridge University many times and my football club has played there quite a few times. We always get a very warm welcome. After Keele, Cambridge University is the second-best university in the world.

The visit to St Hilary's was the second time since the film was on I had been invited to a church. I was glad to get the invite from Rev. David Lake, Rector of Crick, Yelvercroft and Lilbourne – which is in Northamptonshire, just off the M1 – to speak at a special showing of *Marvellous*. The church has had a legacy from a parishioner which they used to establish a new film club in the church itself, which is a marvellous idea. They decided to show *Marvellous* as their first film. Of course, I went. It was very good that Malcolm came with me so that he could give me a lift home afterwards. He came in his Stoke City shirt because Stoke had been playing at Leicester that day. But I went earlier so I could have tea with David. He's a great vicar despite being a Baggies supporter.

MALCOLM
And Rev. David Lake was delighted. He says:

> After watching the film *Marvellous* with Patricia, my wife, we both sensed that the world was a better and more hopeful place. I understood the kind of passion and belief that football inspires, but Neil's faith was like that too. No one seemed more to exemplify Jesus's words about having that childlike trust in order to enter the Kingdom of God.
>
> Neil suggested that his longstanding friend Malcolm might share the evening with him, and, from that moment on, it was all hands to the pump at St Margaret's, Crick. By the time the evening of Saturday, 17 January 2015, came round the excitement was palpable. We had featured in a local newspaper, a live interview had taken place on BBC Radio Northampton and I had even been

selling tickets to people who had stopped me in the streets. It was one of the highlights of my ten years here. At the end of the film more than two hundred people rose to their feet as one and gave Neil Baldwin the most wonderful standing ovation. Everyone found Neil to be as funny, witty and as profound as the film shows him to be.

NEIL

There was then a question-and-answer session. David said to me, 'I've heard, Neil, that you're being made a Freeman of the City of Stoke later this year. Can you tell us exactly what that entitles you to?' I told him what it was: 'I can drive sheep through the city – and enjoy a pint of beer in every pub.'

It was a marvellous evening, the church was packed, and everyone enjoyed the film. When the meeting was over, quite a lot of the parishioners wanted to take photographs with me or get my autograph. Some of them were put on Facebook.

During the questions, I asked David if it was all right for me to go up into the pulpit. I wanted to see how big it is. He said yes, so I did. And they invited me back to preach on Whit Sunday, which was great. I always enjoy preaching in church.

I told everybody that it was good to see the church so full, but I hoped they were all coming back the day after for the Sunday service. After all, it's no good only going to church to see a film, is it? At the end of the evening I said a prayer. They were very kind. They gave me some presents:

a history of the church and, as a joke, the things in the film which my mum didn't want me to have – fruit pastilles and Creme Eggs.

MALCOLM

Neil's request to ascend the steps into the pulpit in the middle of the Q&A, leaving David and me at ground level, was unexpected. But I have learned to expect the unexpected where Neil is involved. The Q&A then began to sound a bit more like a sermon from Neil, but no one minded.

In the audience was Alison Rose Quire, chief executive of an organisation that runs residential facilities, who thought that it would be good to show the film to her organisation's staff conference and have Neil and me there to do a Q&A, which we did. Alison summed up the occasion:

> After seeing the film and hearing Neil and Malcolm speak at a local church, they were an obvious choice to speak at our Care and Community conference. It was like watching a light bulb being switched on. The audience suddenly realised that in many ways we are holding people back by placing limitations on them by virtue of a diagnosis instead of supporting people to have high aspirations and go after their dreams.

NEIL

That was another great occasion. I told them all to be happy and to do what you want to do, because that way you get the most out of life. They seemed to like the film and meeting

Malcolm and me. We have done this a few times now and we make a good team.

MALCOLM

A firm of financial advisers in East Anglia hold an annual meeting for all their clients, and invited Neil to give the keynote speech. Neil and I both felt this wasn't really his cup of tea.

NEIL

I was invited to open the new Watermill School for children with special needs in Burslem. It was a great day, and I unveiled the plaque with my name on it. I gave a talk to encourage the children to do whatever they wanted to do and to enjoy life. Joan Walley, the local Member of Parliament, was also there, and so was Norman Smurthwaite, chairman of Port Vale Football Club, and Tom Pope, one of the players. I had already been up to the school to meet them for lunch, and had been back several times since the opening day, as I am now the patron of the school. The latest time, I had to introduce Prince Andrew's daughter, Princess Beatrice. She was very nice. I told her how often I write to her grandmother, the Queen.

MALCOLM

The head-teacher of Watermill School, Jonathan May, explained why they chose Neil to open the new school and the contribution he makes to the school and the local community:

Neil is now firmly rooted as a friend of the school and indeed has been describing himself as a patron of Watermill, which we are very happy to endorse. He has been for his lunch on around six occasions now. He loves his school dinners and the children always make a great fuss of him. Some of the children that identify with his needs have been heard to ask him if the name-calling was true and what to do about it. I heard him respond that you just ignore it and get on with what you're doing.

It's true, he does know everyone. He came at the end of January to open our school Eco project bringing the Bishop of Stafford, Geoff Annas, with him. It was a fantastic event, almost as good as the opening. The bishop spent the morning in school, he and Neil spoke at the opening and blessed the project. They had lunch and, as usual, Neil tried to blag a lift to Keele University. It was snowing particularly hard, so we took him straight home.

He returned to the circus ring in a cameo appearance in Gandey's Circus when it came to Stoke and he secured us some complimentary tickets. The children and staff really enjoyed seeing him as a clown.

The school feels we owe Neil a lot. He sums up our values and aspirations perfectly. He has gained respect through his humility and interest in being friendly to all. We have learned much from him and his very interesting experiences in life, and of course all the good friends he has.

I was there at the opening along with quite a few of Neil's friends from the Church Army, the Christadelphian Church and even the circus, including Sara, the vice chancellor's PA, and Glynn and Jill Cherry. It was a joyous occasion and showed how much Neil has become a real local celebrity in North Staffordshire.

NEIL
The children even sang a song they had made up especially about me. Here are the words:

I saw the light on the night that I passed by her window;
I saw the flickering shadows of *Match of the Day*.
She was my Stokie.
As Vale scored I watched and went out of my mind.
My, my, my Delilah!
Why, why, why, Delilah?
I could see that girl was no good for me;
But I was lost like a Stoke fan at Vale Park.
At break of day when that Vale match finished, I was waiting;
I crossed the street to her house and she opened the door;
She stood there laughing –
I had Nello with me and she laughed no more.
My, my, my Delilah!
Why, why, why, Delilah?
I could see that girl was no good for me;
Forgive me, Delilah, I just couldn't take any more.

She stood there laughing –
I had Nello with me and she laughed no more.
My, my, my Delilah!
Why, why, why, Delilah?
I could see that girl was no good for me;
Forgive me, Delilah, I just couldn't take any more;
Forgive me, Delilah, I just couldn't take any more.

Not long after the film was broadcast, a group of five Irish musicians based in Dublin, who had never heard of me until they saw the film, formed a special choir called the Nello Irish Choir, saying that they were inspired by the events from my life. A singer and musician with the choir, Ultan Clooney, said, 'Neil's story was heart-warming, positive and so uplifting. It was so funny as well as moving and we were inspired to celebrate this remarkable human man in song.'

A slightly adapted version of this 'Nello song' to the tune of 'Wild Rover' was also sung by the Watermill children at their school's opening:

His name is Nello
He's one of us
And it's fair to say
He's MARVELLOUS

He's Stoke through and through
A Potter so great
Three cheers for Nello
Let's celebrate

CHORUS

Come on Nello,
We all agree,
You're the pride and the joy
Of Watermill school.

Now when Lou Macari
Came up with his plan,
He signed up Nello
As his kit man.

Oh the great Scot Lou
Has often said
Nello was the best signing
He ever made.

CHORUS

Now maybe it's time
Her Majesty
Called on our Nello,
'Come and see me.'

He'll kneel before her
And with delight
Mister Neil Baldwin
Will be a knight.

CHORUS

I was invited by Newcastle College to do a talk to students who have problems, and to join an assembly at the St John Fisher Catholic School. I was also asked to meet Keele students who don't go out and meet people, undergrads who are lonely. They come and see me.

One of the nicest things has been that I was invited to open the new ground of Leek County School Old Boys (CSOB) Football Club and to be their manager for their first game.

I gave the team talk for the start of the game and I told them, 'To win games you need to score goals.' And the team were 3–0 up at half-time, when I gave them another talk and said, 'I want more goals from you.' And the final result was 5–0, so it worked.

MALCOLM

The CSOB goalkeeper, Phil Bruce, recalls:

Neil was the very first official guest at Poynton's Park. The lads had got to know him; he had been to our Halloween Party. After the game we took him to the Black Lion pub, where players had their pictures taken with him and he signed menus.

I'd known Neil for about two years; I just fell in love with the guy. You could talk to him about anything. He phones me most days, and he asked me to be a coach for the Neil Baldwin Football Club, which I'm delighted to do, so we have training sessions every Friday afternoon.

Bolstered by the effect of the film, the Neil Baldwin Football Club goes from strength to strength. I think Neil is going to find it a challenge to give all the players who have now signed up for his club a game.

Jack Harding is a current player in his fourth season playing for NBFC. He recalls:

> It was my first weekend at uni when I met Neil. He said, 'Do you like playing football?' And I've been playing for NBFC ever since. I prefer playing for NBFC because I don't want a whole load of football club politics, although I have played for the Keele University fourth team. Neil is just part of the family here. It's a two-way thing: he looks after us and we look after him. We played a game against St John's Theology College and other teams.
>
> I think my first game was against Exeter University and we lost 7–1. It was a bit of a mismatch.
>
> When giving him a lift on one occasion I was a bit taken aback when he suddenly asked me to pull up and 'buy me some bird seed'. He has a warm personality. I went down to Imperial College to play in the Neil Baldwin Cup.

Yes, the Neil Baldwin Cup, started by Neil Baldwin and his old friend Neil Mosley, the head of sport at Imperial College, is still going. Neil Mosley tells me, 'Last time he was here he said he wanted to meet the Imperial College chaplain, Andrew, so Andrew came along and Neil worked the usual Baldwin magic on him.'

Neil Mosley has been having cancer treatment, and, typically, Neil Baldwin phones him regularly to find out how he is. 'Are you any better now? I'm praying for you,' he says.

NEIL

We did really well this year and won the cup. We won the first game 9–0.

MALCOLM

Who was that against?

NEIL

My second team.

MALCOLM

These days Neil spends a lot of time in the Keele University Sports Centre, which has become one of his established bases. Richard Whitehead works there:

> I've known Neil for twelve years; he has an unofficial office here. When he doesn't turn up we want to know where he is. It's great to see returning students who remember Neil.
>
> Over the years he has given many students the chance to play football. This includes different standards and all groups; they come and train every Friday and the Neil Baldwin Football Club is a registered society in the Students' Union.

I know he's been to big clubs such as Manchester City because I've seen photographs of Neil with Robbie Fowler, Kevin Keegan, David James and Steve McMahon.

Jack adds:

His team talks can be hilarious. He'll just shout instructions. He shouted, 'Sykes, get the ball' on one occasion when Sykes was actually on the bench. Once, when I was getting changed, he said 'Jack, you're a sex beast' when I took my shirt off. That has stuck as a nickname ever since.

Richard adds, 'When the local kids come here for the local Football Tournament, you can hear them saying, "Is that Neil Baldwin?" We have an annual Christmas meal, when Neil will tell them all what he thinks.'

On 26 January 2015, Neil attended the ordination of Bishop Libby Lane, the new Bishop of Stockport and the first ever female bishop in the Church of England. There is a picture of Neil, Bishop Lane and the Archbishop of York.

In March 2015, Gandey's Circus arrived in town on the car park of the Britannia Stadium. In an astute marketing move, they invited Nello the Clown to return to the ring. It played to full houses, and Nello got the biggest cheer when he took to the ring. As ever it didn't faze him at all.

At one point the ringmaster says, 'So you've made a return to the ring, Nello. What's it like?' And he replies, 'Marvellous!' It brought the house down.

Neil accepted an invitation to be in the pantomime at the Regent Theatre at Hanley in winter 2015–16. Once again, he is expected to be an important magnet for bringing in audiences.

Meanwhile back at Keele, the Neil method of making friends hadn't changed. One new friend was a young man who had come to work at the university, Brad Gurney, who told me:

I first met Mr Baldwin when some people who I work with were interviewing him to go on the Keele website. I'd heard the name Nello talked about around The Britannia Stadium and by various other people, but never quite understood the history and legacy that he had. So there I was, sitting quietly, waiting for him to come in to be interviewed.

He came into the chapel, sat down, looked at everyone, then turned his attentions to me and gave me a firm nod; I nodded back.

'Who're you, then?' he asked.

Hesitantly, I replied, 'Oh I'm just Brad – big Stoke fan, though.'

There was something about this man that intrigued me. As I listened to his responses that he gave to the questions in the interview, I wanted to know more. This guy seemed like he'd seen it all and that nothing seemed to surprise him. So I did what I wanted, I got to know more.

I often spent my lunch hours talking to him

about the Stoke matches that had been played and the ones that we had coming up. We'd talk about various players and different performances. It wasn't long before the errands started: 'Can you nip to the paper shop for me?'; 'Can you go and get me a Diet Coke?'; 'Can you go and post these for me?' I don't know what it was about him, but I just couldn't say no, it was as if he was asking them as rhetorical questions – he must've known I was going to say yes. If it was anyone else I'd have probably said, 'Go and do it yourself, I've been bloody working all day!' But no, this wasn't possible with Neil (and still isn't).

Within the space of a few weeks, I was named assistant manager of his football team, I attended evenings with [football manager] Barry Fry and various other sporting icons.

CHAPTER ELEVEN

THE PILGRIMS

NEIL

It's getting difficult to fit everything into the diary. I get invited to all sorts of things, and people come to the Potteries especially to meet me. I like all that.

In December I was invited to give one of the awards at the BBC TV Midlands Sports Personality of the Year at Villa Park in Birmingham. I was pleased that it was held at Villa Park because that was the ground where I made my appearance for Stoke City. I was giving the Newcomer of the Year Award. I went down on the train with Malcolm and I was recognised at Stoke Station and on the train by people who had seen the film and said how marvellous it was. When we arrived at Villa Park, I was very surprised to see Lou Macari there. Lou didn't let on why he was there, but it turned out that they were also giving me a surprise award, presented by Lou. It was a great night which I really enjoyed.

MALCOLM

On the train down, Neil told me that the previous evening he had been at a function with the police in Stoke-on-Trent. He had been asked to say a few words at the end so I asked him what he had said.

NEIL

I told the police that I pray for them every night and that the cuts that David Cameron is introducing in the police services are disgraceful. I got a great round of applause. I think Malcolm wasn't sure I ought to have said that but it was what I thought.

MALCOLM

It's not surprising that Neil's comments went down so well with the local police force. But on the way, I told Neil that as this was a televised sporting occasion, not a political occasion, perhaps it would be a good idea not to have a go at David Cameron. Neil said he understood and completely agreed.

Neil gave his award as planned, and we were both surprised at the end when they got Lou Macari up on the stage. It was only then that we realised why Lou was there – to give Neil his special award. Neil got interviewed on stage; the presenter asked if he had been busy since *Marvellous* had been on television. Neil replied, 'Yes, I have. I have something on almost every day. For example, last night I was with the police in Stoke, and I told them that what David Cameron is doing to the police force...'

The presenter looked a little uncomfortable, but Neil will do what he fancies doing. When I looked at the recorded highlights of the evening on television later, I noticed that they hadn't included Neil's contributions to current political debates.

At New Street Station, another passenger asked Neil if he was Neil Baldwin. Hearing that he was, she asked if she could take a selfie with Neil to send to her partner. She had absolutely loved the film, and her partner would never believe that she had met the real Nello at the station.

NEIL

People now recognise me all the time. I went to Beverley in East Yorkshire for a Service of Ordination in Beverley Minster. When the man in the small hotel where I was staying found out who I was, he was very excited, and it even ended up as a story on the front page of the local paper with a picture of himself and me.

At Hull Station on the way home, I saw a young man looking at me. He came forward and asked if I was Neil Baldwin. When I said yes he wanted a selfie photograph to send to his friends because he said they would not believe he had met Neil Baldwin on Hull Station. He was a student returning to Nottingham University and we had a good chat on the train.

I was also invited as a guest at the BBC Sports Personality of the Year ceremony in Glasgow. I went with my friend Brad from Keele. I was one of the guests of honour and it was great to enter the arena along the red carpet.

MALCOLM

I turned on the TV to watch the BBC News channel that evening when they did an outside broadcast from the Sports Personality of the Year. The very first people I saw were Neil and Brad walking along the red carpet behind the presenter who was doing a preview of the evening's event.

NEIL

It was a great night. Gary Lineker, who is the President of the Neil Baldwin Football Club, saw me and gave a cheerful wave. I was sitting near to Judy Murray and Susan Boyle, who gave me a kiss. It was great to be part of the ceremony.

Brad loved it too.

MALCOLM

Brad certainly did. Here's his account of the occasion:

> By November, it was routine for me to go down to Neil at lunchtime, sit with him, eat our food and give him a lift to the Sports Centre. One day he produced these two shiny tickets that read 'BBC Sports Personality of the Year 2014'. I'd watched this on telly plenty of times before, the first ticket was addressed to Neil 'Nello' Baldwin and the second to 'Bradley Gumbey' (it's Gurney, not Gumbey, thanks Nello, that name has stuck for life). 'We're going to Glasgow, Brad!'
>
> Yes Neil, we certainly are…
>
> So there we are, Saturday, 13 December, in the bitterly cold morning waiting for our train. I

hadn't got a small suitcase, so I had to borrow a friend's. The only trouble was, it was bright pink. As soon as Nello laid eyes on it, he just laughed at me. There I am, walking round Stoke, Crewe and Glasgow train stations with this bright pink suitcase, getting very funny looks from both men and women. But we didn't care. We were going to Glasgow to meet our sporting heroes!

Neil was like a kid in a sweet shop, we both were, we were on countdown now. Only another eight hours until we were meeting people we had seen on the telly and had heard about through various sporting competitions.

We got to the venue and showed them our tickets. 'Right this way Mr Gumbey.' I was too polite to say, 'It's Gurney!' I didn't care though, you could call me every name under the sun and it wouldn't affect me, I was at the Sports Personality Awards!

Neil and I met various people such as Susan Boyle, Robbie Savage, Sir Chris Hoy, Gabby Logan, Clare Balding, Kenny Dalglish and Jonny Wilkinson. Every famous person Neil met, he introduced himself with the same line, 'Hello, I'm Neil Baldwin, have you seen my film? It was called *Marvellous* on BBC2. It's on again Christmas Day, so watch it if you haven't seen it and watch it again if you have.'

NEIL

I was also invited by Lou to go with him to the National Journalism Awards in London. Pete Bowker was there and *Marvellous* was getting an award.

We went down on the train from Stoke-on-Trent. When we arrived at Euston, we were walking down the platform when we heard two ladies, and one of them was saying: 'It is him, yes, I am sure it's him.' They then came forward with a camera and asked if they could have a picture. Lou smiled and said, of course, and they handed the camera to Lou and asked him if he would mind taking a photograph of them with Neil Baldwin. I think Lou thought he was the one who had been spotted. So I'm now more famous than Lou.

At the ceremony, Lou arranged for me to be wearing the chicken suit.

MALCOLM

Lou told me: 'After the ceremony we had time to spare so I said to Neil, "Would you like to go to the cinema? You can choose the film." He jumped at the chance and chose *Paddington*.'

NEIL

I loved it. Lou fell asleep which meant he missed a lot of a great film.

Since the film, I've been invited to a lot of sporting dinners and lunches for 'an evening with Neil Baldwin' type events. There's usually a clip from the film and a Q and A with Lou, Terry Conroy or Malcolm. I suppose I'm a celebrity on the after-dinner circuit.

One of these was at Alsager Golf Club where two of the members present were Andrew Edwards, the local undertaker and Stoke City supporter who's an old friend of mine, and the former Stoke City striker, Jimmy Greenhoff. Jimmy was such a great player that I let him sign his autograph in the front of my Bible.

Andrew's golf must have improved a lot since that time in the Isle of Man when he broke a glass table practising his golf swing. He probably practised with that children's golf kit I brought him. He is a very nice man and organises very good funerals. The funerals of Sir Stanley Matthews and Mary Gandey were marvellous, even though they were very sad.

One of the things I'm most pleased about was meeting a young Tottenham Hotspur supporter called Reuben who has sadly been ill with a form of cancer. He watched *Marvellous* on television and loved it. His mum wrote to Stoke City to ask if there was any chance of meeting me. He wasn't well enough to travel up to the Potteries.

As it happens, Stoke City were playing away at Spurs a few weeks later. The two clubs made all the arrangements for me to go down on the supporter's coach and meet Reuben before the game. Spurs looked after us both and gave us a nice meal. Tiger Aspect were wonderful and gave the clown shoes and a clown outfit that was actually used in the film for me to present to Reuben. He loved it and it was a really good day.

Reuben and I have kept in touch since then. He also came with his mum to see us play for the Baldwin Cup at Imperial College, and he won the penalty competition. I am pleased to say that he is feeling much better. That's one of the very best things that's happened to me since the film.

Brad came along with me that time.

MALCOLM

Brad was delighted to be asked. He says:

> One lunchtime, he said, 'Eh Brad, come here! I've got some news for you! I'm going down to London to watch Stoke play Spurs and meet a little lad who's seen my film, he's got cancer and wants to meet me.'
>
> 'Bloody hell Neil, that's great! That's this weekend isn't it?' I replied.
>
> 'Oh, ah, it is, and you're coming with me.' I thought he was winding me up, why would he invite me? Yeah, he knew I was a Stoke fan, but why wouldn't he take someone else? I obviously jumped at the chance.
>
> So we went down, we got the coach on a very early Sunday morning, he introduced me to the Stoke team, the backroom staff and various people he knew. I couldn't believe it.

NEIL

Two city councillors in Stoke proposed that Neil Baldwin and the great Gordon Banks should be made Freemen of the City of Stoke-on-Trent. It was carried unanimously. It's a marvellous honour. Can you imagine what my mum and dad would have thought of that? I'm really pleased to have been given it on the same day as the great Gordon Banks, who is one of my footballing heroes.

I will be entitled to drive a herd of sheep through the city centre, and I'm planning to do that to raise money for charity.

MALCOLM

The city council chose the annual *Sentinel* Sports Awards dinner for the City of Stoke and surrounding areas to make the award. *The Sentinel* is the local paper, and several local sporting awards are presented.

After taking the long and antiquated oath of allegiance which new Freemen are required to make, it was not clear that an oral response was expected but Neil stepped forward and said: 'I'd like to respond on behalf of myself and Gordon.' I don't know whether he consulted Gordon Banks first, but Gordon didn't object. After saying thank you, and how honoured he was, Neil randomly cracked a joke about the Chinese telephone system which rather passed over the heads of those present. But nobody minded. Everyone there shared Neil's pride and recognised the contribution which he and *Marvellous* has made to promoting the City of Stoke-on-Trent.

Lou commented in a media interview that he hoped Neil 'doesn't think that the Freedom of Stoke-on-Trent means that he can go and purchase anything in any shop without paying for it.'

On the same day that the city council decided to make Neil a Freeman of the City, the Neil Baldwin Football Club were playing a game at Rocester FC. Neil rang me to say that he was taking a squad of sixteen to the match. I asked him what he was doing with the remaining 108. 'Resting them,' was the reply.

Zara and I turned up to the game at Rocester to see a television crew in attendance. When I asked Neil who they were, in that kind of matter-of-fact way he has of taking these things in his stride, he just said. 'Oh, that's Norwegian television.' I didn't even bother to ask how it had come about. You just come to expect these things with Neil.

Radio 5 Live were also there and recorded an interview with myself and Neil for a piece the following morning about him being given the Freeman of the City of Stoke.

About five minutes before the end of the game, the floodlights failed, with Rocester beating NBFC by eight goals to two. It was fairly obvious that the match would not be resumed.

We waited in the darkness outside the clubhouse, when suddenly there was a cheer which came from the direction of the pitch. We couldn't see anything. The PA announcer then said, 'And the third goal from NBFC, scored by the man himself, Mr Neil Baldwin.'

It transpired that Neil had insisted on going onto the pitch to take a penalty which he had scored – perhaps not entirely surprisingly as it was being taken in total darkness, which doesn't help even the best of keepers. But it will, no doubt, go down in his records as yet another goal he has scored for his team.

NEIL

I was not too worried about the score because we hadn't played too many games that season. But at least I scored. I always do. It was a marvellous night because it was the same day that I had been given the Freeman of the City of Stoke-on-Trent.

MALCOLM

In December, as National Chair of the Football Supporters' Federation, I attended a press conference in the National Football Museum in Manchester given by Clive Efford, MP, the Shadow Minister of Sport, who was outlining Labour's policy on football in advance of the general election. Television crews and journalists were covering the event.

At the end of the press conference, Clive beckoned me into a corner to have a quiet word. I was expecting him to say something about the policy, perhaps that they needed a little help on the detail and would we be willing to do that? Far from it. What Clive actually said was: 'Would there be any chance of the Parliamentary football team having a game against the Neil Baldwin Football Club?'

Of course, I said, I'm sure that Neil would be absolutely delighted. I mentioned it to Neil. Naively (how long have I known him?) I didn't expect him to start the ball rolling. But a few days later I got a phone call from Neil.

'What was the name of that MP who wanted a football match against NBFC?'

'Clive Efford.'

'Because I've rang the House of Commons and got through to that woman who knew nothing about it.'

'What woman?'

'Harriet Harman.'

Neil had rung the House of Commons and asked to be put

through to the Labour party spokesperson on sport. Instead of being put through to the Shadow Minister of Sport he had been put through to Clive Efford's boss, the Shadow Secretary of State, Harriet Harman. If most of the rest of us were to ring the Commons in these circumstances we would probably get to speak to a member of the MP's office staff, but Neil had been put straight through to Harriet, who didn't know anything about the football match.

A few weeks later I saw Clive again at the National Arboretum, where there was an unveiling of a memorial for the footballers who had fought in the First World War. He told me that Harriet had buttonholed him on the floor at the House of Commons saying: have you sorted out that football match, because I've got this chap who has been on the phone to me wanting something done about it.

Neil doesn't let the grass grow under his feet.

NEIL

It will be marvellous when NBFC play the Parliamentary team. I hope that Boris Johnson plays, because if he does, I shall get one of the players to kick him.

MALCOLM

Neil's old friend Terry Conroy, along with businessmen Mike Finnigan and David Brownsword, met at the end of December 2014. David said:

> An idea was put to Neil up for an event called
> 'An Audience with Neil Baldwin' to celebrate his
> life to date and to let others have the first hand

experience of what a wonderful man he is. A very important by-product of the proposed event was to raise money for good causes. Neil, with a big smile, was totally hooked and excited.

Seven weeks later the event, with just fifty guests, was held at Roundhouse Restaurant in Hayfield, situated in the delightful Peak District. Terry and I joined Neil for a Q and A. David summed it up:

> It was crowned by Neil doing a wonderful duet with the talented singer/songwriter Beatie Wolfe. Neil was singing along, or trying to (without rehearsing the lyrics), to Beatie's charity single 'Wish'. £7000 was made for the nominated good causes. (You can listen to that at www.youtube. com/watch?v=nkQA-tgU2N4.)

There are now plans to repeat the event elsewhere, possibly as far afield as Glasgow and Kent. David and his friends have also set up a website about Neil: www.marvellousneilbaldwin. com

NEIL

It was a great day, and I'm so pleased we raised so much money for charity. Beatie was really pleased to have the chance to do a duet with me. Not too many artists get that chance. Phil Dowd, the Premier League referee, was there and I told him the penalty he gave to Wayne Rooney a few days before was wrong. But he's a great referee really, even though I think he's a Vale fan. I fixed up a couple of games for NBFC. It will be marvellous if we can do more shows in other places to raise money for charity.

MALCOLM

Despite all this activity, Neil retains his regular presence at Keele. Lucy O'Dwyer, the 2015 President of the Athletic Union, described her daily requests from Neil:

> Every morning I walk past Neil, he will be sat downstairs in the Students' Union and will ask either for a pen or cappuccino. Then, in the afternoon, he will ask for an Oxo cube (always beef) stirred into hot water which, I presume, is his mid-afternoon snack.
>
> He will then go and sit in the Sports Centre proclaiming me to be a 'funny girl' (although, I'd argue the Oxo cube in hot water is funnier) with a tendency to get very passionate when discussing politics – 'It's Cameron's fault we're in this mess!'
>
> [Describing last year's Sports Centre Christmas party] He presented us all with a pair of black socks that looked suspiciously like they'd all come from the same multi-pack. I don't think Neil agrees with Secret Santa...

NEIL

Lucy is a very good friend of mine. She looks after me and I look after her. I've known all the athletic union presidents in the last fifty years, and she's one of the best.

MALCOLM

Alex Clifford, who graduated in 2014 recalled:

The first time I met Neil was during a night out in the Students' Union building. It was close to 1 a.m. and I had popped down to the Kiln for some cheesy chips and gravy. I then heard a strange squawk in my direction, and I turned to see an older man walking towards me. 'Hey you, would you mind getting me some chips?' he asked. I said 'absolutely', got into the queue and sat with Neil as we munched on our chips. And thus I was introduced to the wonder that is Neil Baldwin.

In my time since, I've provided Neil with lifts from the SU building to the Sports Centre, helped him set up stalls at Freshers' Fair for his football club, and (attempted) to provide him with the whereabouts of Joe Turner, president at the time that I was VP of welfare in 2013, another 'very good friend' of Neil's.

I'll always remember Neil as Santa during the early Winterfest (Winter ball) parties during my time, and his famous line from *Marvellous* about helping a girl, to prevent her from committing suicide.

Neil was always around campus, attending all the events he could manage. He always liked to come to the Union Awards night to see Societies and Clubs be rewarded for doing well over the year, and even managed to turn up on the door and get entry when the Head of Student Support couldn't! Maybe one day he'll be asked to stand up and make a speech about the many clubs and societies he's seen progress over the years.

Declan Carey, a third year student says:

After attending a training session, Neil texted me about a match at Oxford coming up. He tried to tempt me with the prospect of an Apple Sourz shot if I received Man of the Match – what a hero! After this, Neil never forgot me and he continues to say hello to this day, chatting with me every time he sees me.

I did some research and read Francis Beckett's piece in *The Guardian* and began to understand that there was more to Neil than I had anticipated. The man who never forgot to say hello, and who had been at Keele forever, actually had a fascinating past which I ashamedly had known nothing about despite knowing him for a year.

Prior to the showing of *Marvellous*, Keele alumni officer John Easom generously invited me to attend a meal with Neil and Malcolm Clarke in the Sneyd Arms. I felt I was being too quiet, so often tried to add my own experience into the conversation, but I felt like I was sitting at a table of Keele giants who had more stories than I could contemplate.

That night I just listened. Neil and Malcolm

told me all about the filming process and some of the key moments which would be shown in the film. I asked Neil how he felt about Toby Jones portraying him in the film. 'He was brilliant,' he said. 'But what a scruff he looked!'

I still see Neil all over campus and he still says hello and stops for a chat. It's almost like the film and fame never happened and he is just a normal bloke sitting around campus. That is until he reminds me of his aim to get an MBE and it all becomes real.

For Neil, nothing's changed except that, as he puts it, he's got famous. He still makes new friends in exactly the same way as he used to do, and he treats everyone the same way. Brad, a new friend himself, sees that clearly:

When I look back on the things I've done since meeting Neil, it really makes me smile. I'm from a working-class family, raised by a single parent and I never had much growing up, but that didn't matter to Neil, you could have all the money in the world and he wouldn't care. To Neil, people are people and that's all that matters. In his eyes, I'm no different to Gary Lineker or any of his sporting idols, because it doesn't matter how you are viewed in the public eye, whether you're a TV presenter or work at Keele, people are people. I've had some amazing experiences with Neil, I'll cherish the memories for life and hopefully we will have many more together. We are like Stoke's version of Ant and Dec (apart from our guts and good looks). So thank you Neil.

NEIL

In March 2015 the Neil Baldwin Football Club was invited to play an evening away game under floodlights against Gresley FC, a Derbyshire club who play in the Evo-Stik League. This took my football club to a new level. There was a £5 admission charge and the official attendance was eighty-one. There was a glossy match programme, which included an article about the film, listed the Neil Baldwin FC team and showed it including former Stoke City star Danny Higginbotham. There was a big article about Danny, and another about my friend Uriah Rennie, who I got to referee the match again.

Unfortunately, Danny couldn't play. But I will select him for a future game. And it was great that my old friend Macca, former Stoke City goal-scoring star Mike Sheron, made his debut as a substitute for my team.

Both teams lined up to be formally presented to me before the kick-off and I had an interview on the pitch with the PA announcer. Everyone wants to talk to me.

MALCOLM

It also included a new experience for me. I had been a director of the Neil Baldwin Football Club for over forty years, but during that time, the board had never met! I had often asked Neil about this and he had repeatedly promised to arrange a meeting. But now the Chairman of Gresley Rovers had invited the directors of the Neil Baldwin Football Club into the boardroom and to sit in the directors' area. So after four decades of waiting, I fulfilled my first official function as a director of NBFC. I thought it would never happen. Dreams are made of this.

NEIL

It's been difficult to find a time for a board meeting, but the club is being run well by me as the manager, coach and kit manager. Malcolm knows that, but he just wanted to go into a boardroom and I'm pleased that I've given him the chance to do that.

MALCOLM

The game itself did not start very well for NBFC who were 3–0 down within about half an hour, one of the goals being scored by former Stoke City player, 'Freezer' Goodfellow.

NEIL

Myself (as manager), Phil (as my coach), and Brad (who I've appointed as assistant coach), were in the dugout, so that's a pretty good team. We were all listed in the programme. It was a poor start so we had to tell the team a few home-truths at half-time.

MALCOLM

Things went better in the second half, perhaps because NBFC were playing downhill on Gresley's famous slope. Uriah gave a free kick to NBFC about twenty-five yards from goal. Up stepped Mike Sheron to curl a beautifully

247

taken free kick around the wall and into the top corner of the net. Talk about rolling back the years!

NEIL

That was a great goal by Macca. I would have been proud to score that one.

MALCOLM

Throughout the game, the crowd could hear the constant encouragement of Phil, the NBFC coach, followed a few second later by the same instruction being given in a rather deeper voice from the back of the dugout.

Phil: 'Go on, tuck in there, don't give him room...'

Neil: 'Tuck in there, don't give him room.'

Phil: 'Get down there on the overlap...'

Neil: 'Get down there on the overlap.'

The game ended with a 3–1 defeat for NBFC. Or did it? After the final whistle Neil came onto the pitch to take his customary 'penalty', although unlike the game at Rocester, on this occasion not in total darkness! He put it into the corner of the net with his trademark celebratory shake of the fist.

NEIL

That was a great penalty – right in the corner. Macca had a goal disallowed for offside, but it should have been allowed, which, together with my penalty meant that the score will go down as a three-all draw.

MALCOLM

I chatted to a few members of the crowd. Two guys had told me that they had seen the film on television, had seen the match advertised locally, and felt that they just had to come down and see the real Neil Baldwin Football Club, even though they were not regular attendees at Gresley FC. Another lady told me that the film had changed her life, in that she now has a completely different attitude towards problems and issues in her own life.

Similarly, a fellow Stoke City supporter, who I didn't previously know, told me that watching the film had made him re-evaluate the way he looked at and dealt with problems of his own and put them into perspective. The line 'I wanted to be happy, so I decided to be,' has struck a particular chord with a lot of people.

In fact, one of the most extraordinary consequences of the broadcasting of *Marvellous* has been the number of ordinary people who, like those two, have said that watching the film has changed their lives, and a number of them have contacted Neil, usually through Stoke City FC or Keele University.

Some have contacted Neil simply to come and visit him. Michelle Wren, from Liverpool said:

> When I watched *Marvellous* it changed my life. I made my family and friends watch it and it changed their lives too. Neil is an example of how to live life. He inspired me so much I rang up Keele University to see if the Neil Baldwin Football Club was still running and if it would be

possible to come and meet him. They said yes, so I brought my parents, who also loved the film, and we went to Keele to meet Neil.

I was worried that it was strange to just go and meet this man who had inspired me so much, but then I thought, 'What would Neil Baldwin do?' If Neil Baldwin watched the film and liked the character he would just go and meet them, so I did and it was lovely. So now I like to think, 'He's a very good friend of mine.' And when I am thinking of whether or not to do something I simply say to myself, 'What would Neil Baldwin do?' There might be 'only one Neil Baldwin' but I think the world would be better if there were a few more.

NEIL

Michelle and her family also came to see me as 'Nello' in Gandey's Circus, where they met Malcolm, and Michelle and her friends also came to see me and Malcolm at St Mark's church in Birkenhead. They are lovely people.

MALCOLM

Brian Jeeves took up writing about football late in life:

I, like millions of other TV viewers, have been completely transfixed by Peter Bowker's portrayal of Neil in the wonderful film *Marvellous*. I analysed the film several times and on each occasion I saw something that had passed me by during previous viewings. Nevertheless, one line stood out above all others: 'I wanted to be happy, so I decided to be.'

Could it really be that simple? This is quite an inspirational man we are dealing with and a ninety-minute film wasn't going to be enough. I needed more. I simply had to meet him, so on a wing and a prayer I wrote to Nello c/o Stoke City Football Club, and within a week I had a reply waiting for me. So it was that I travelled up to Stoke on 1 November 2014, reporting on Stoke City versus West Ham United but, more important than that, meeting the famous Nello, who was sitting on the wall opposite the ticket office. I am not generally affected by nervousness, but as I approached I felt slightly in awe of this man before me.

Neil held court with almost every Potters fan that came our way. Perhaps it was blind faith, but each of them seemed lifted by his words of wisdom. Blimey, how I could have done with a Nello pep talk each week before watching my beloved but enormously frustrating Southend United, I thought.

Nello has led an enriched life which has taken many varied pathways. Sure, doors have opened along the way, but then again you make your own luck – from circus clown to film star via Stoke City kit man, of course. But rather than wallow in his own accomplishments Neil positively encourages folk to share in his optimistic aura, giving advice and unquestionably wanting people to find happiness, even if it means sharing his own with them.

Do things just happen for Neil or does he make them happen? Maybe if we could be all be a bit more like Neil life would be enhanced, we'd be happy and all get along better. But then again, could anyone else be like him? After all, there's only one Neil Baldwin!

Brian's visit to meet Neil had a further spin-off. He told Neil about a friend of his, Rev. Alex Summers, who had been undergoing hospital treatment for heart problems. Neil tried to contact Alex, having told Brian, 'I'll go to visit him.' Alex takes up the story:

I was so touched that he was willing to travel to visit someone who he had never met and who was unwell that I decided I should honour him by visiting him. I was moved by him showing concern and keeping me in his prayers. It was one of the most poignant films I have ever seen, so lovely, but also so ordinary. Neil is the kind of person who could have been discarded by society, but has touched so many lives.

When I went to see him to say thank you for his concern, it almost felt like a pilgrimage. I felt like I had known Neil all my life. And I think there is a real sense in which everyone who watches the film feels they know him. I'll never be as selfless as he is and I find him to be a wonderfully inspiring person.

When I visited him at Keele he took me to the Vice-Chancellor's office. When I visit hospitals, the dog collar almost gives you permission to go where I want to. It felt like that with Neil at Keele – by being Neil he could go anywhere and everyone knew him.

'Pilgrimage' seems an appropriate word to describe these journeys to meet Neil.

NEIL

Brian and Alex are lovely people. Brian has written some good books about football which he kindly sent to me. It is always great to meet a fellow minister of God.

Did you know I was treated to £25 worth of Wrights pie vouchers after being randomly photographed tucking in to one of their lovely pies at the Britannia Stadium, during our exciting 2–2 draw with West Ham? That was a real piece of luck, although my mum wouldn't have thought much of it. She probably wouldn't have let me eat them.

And another thing. When the general election came round, our local MPs were really glad I was a Labour man. Paul Farrelly in Newcastle-under-Lyme and Tristram Hunt in Stoke Central both asked me to endorse them for their election leaflets. I've seen Tristram's leaflet – very good it was too. I was glad, after all my time at Keele, to be able to help Labour's education spokesman.

MALCOLM

Everything's changed, yet nothing's changed. Neil Baldwin is the same man I met all those years ago in 1964 who said 'Welcome to Keele. I'm Neil Baldwin.' He goes to the same places, talks to the same people, works in the same way. More people know about it, that's all.

Jonathan Hughes, whom we last met in the late 1990s, when he was rather hoping Neil could fix him a trial with Stoke City, sees that very clearly. He says:

> After leaving Keele in 2000, I didn't give Neil a huge amount of thought until I watched *Marvellous* with my wife.
>
> It was probably three months after watching the film that a Norwegian friend of mine visited with his partner and as part of the itinerary we arranged to go down to Keele with a few of our old mates to have a bit of a reminisce. Having parked up in the car park outside the Union we walked straight through the doors to an almost unrecognisable building. With one exception... Neil sat at one of the tables having his lunch. I couldn't believe it.

NEIL

Pete Bowker and I went to Lambeth Palace for the Sandford St Martin religious broadcasting awards ceremony. *Marvellous* didn't win this one, but we came a very good second, and I got lots of autographs and pictures from people like the Bishop of Leeds.

Malcolm and I went to Gresley FC for their end-of-season awards dinner. I had to present a new award called the 'Clown of the Dressing Room' to the player who had contributed most to dressing room spirit. They made us both honorary vice-presidents, and gave us a club badge and tie.

I also went to the official Stoke City end-of-season awards dinner and got 'Fan of the Season.'

MALCOLM

I didn't go to that one, and neither did most of Neil's friends, because the tickets cost £300 pus VAT – it's targeted at corporate sponsors, not ordinary fans. Stoke City must be the only club where you can buy a season ticket for a lot less than a ticket to the awards dinner.

NEIL

Lots of good things are happening. The Stoke City Old Boys Association, the organisation of former players of Stoke City, has made me its president. Leek Ladies FC has also made me its president. I'm off to another concert by Beatie Wolf in Liverpool and the Bishop of Birkenhead is coming too. I've been asked to appear as a vicar in the TV programme *Granchester*. In September 2015 I'll be filming *Songs of Praise* for BBC TV with Aled Jones. I'm sure he will be looking forward to meeting me.

And I'm working on plans for my seventieth birthday party next year. I haven't decided what they'll be yet. But it'll be a very good party. You can be sure of that.

AFTERWORD

By Francis Beckett

I usually avoid watching the BAFTAs on television. There's something smug and patronising about the film industry congratulating itself in public. And you always know that what you're allowed to watch, glittering and expensive though it is, is only a foretaste of the real party to come, when we *sans culottes* have been sent to our suburban beds.

But I made an exception on 10 May 2015, when the film about Neil Baldwin, *Marvellous*, was up for three awards: Best Single Drama, Best Leading Actor (Toby Jones as Neil) and Best Supporting Actress (Gemma Jones as Mary Baldwin, Neil's mother). I knew that Neil, Malcolm and Lou Macari were to be there with the cast and crew, and there was always the chance of getting a glimpse of Neil hovering near the camera, just as there is every year when you watch the Boat Race on television.

257

And I felt I had a stake in it. If I hadn't profiled Neil in *The Guardian*, the film would never have been made. A lifetime of writing and journalism, seventeen books, more newspaper features than I can count, and I don't think I've ever written anything that had such far-reaching results.

That afternoon, Neil and Malcolm travelled down to London and went to the 'boutique hotel' that the film company had booked them into, looked around the luxuriously quirky book-lined bedrooms, and wondered what was in the 'Love Box' they could buy for £25. 'Is it cigars in there?' asked Neil, but it turned out only to be fair-trade condoms, massage lotion, lubricant and vibe couples rings, so they passed on it.

Malcolm, Neil and Lou went on to the Drury Lane Theatre and joined the cast and crew. Watching at home, I cheered spontaneously when Gemma Jones won. If anyone ever deserved an acting award, she did. She had got inside the skin of her character.

Toby Jones just missed out on Best Actor – he was up against some very strong competition. And then there was the big one: Best Single Drama. The tension was unbearable. Malcolm told me, 'It's worse than a penalty shootout in a football final.' Then they heard the words '...and the winner is absolutely...' and they thought something else had won, but then they heard, '...*Marvellous*.' The leading members of the cast and the production and creative team, and Neil and Malcolm and Lou, walked onto the platform.

Writer Peter Bowker made a short, graceful speech. 'The film is a celebration about the positive contribution everyone can make. It's a celebration of diversity and community and the spirit of optimism. These are values worth fighting for, more so now than ever.' Peter was as horrified by the general election result three days earlier as I was, and as I know Neil was, and he was determined to say so: 'Thank you, BAFTA. At least one vote went the right way this week.'

But, towards the end of his speech, I could see what was about to happen – and the rising panic Peter must be feeling. Most viewers would not have realised, but everyone who has known Neil over the years could tell the signs. Neil was making it clear to Peter that he wanted to speak; and Peter was thinking, 'This is live television, we have to be really disciplined and keep it short – what's going to happen if I let Neil get to the microphone?'

But he had to make an instant decision. He said, 'And it won't surprise anyone that Neil would like to say a word.' Not for the first time, everyone underestimated Neil. He was as tight and disciplined as any professional, and less self-indulgent than most.

He said, 'I would like to thank everyone in *Marvellous* for how great it was. I would also like to thank my friends at Keele University, my football team, and Phil Bruce. It's been great to be here and I thank the Lord. And, I'm very pleased that the queen is still going strong.'

And, somehow, that legitimised the whole tinselly show, for hundreds of people. Stoke City supporters, Keele University graduates and staff, Oxford and Cambridge Boat Race enthusiasts (especially Cambridge ones), circus clowns and performers, curates and vicars and bishops – they all felt for the first time that they owned a piece of the BAFTAs.

The television coverage ended and the stars and presenter

Graham Norton went on to their real celebration: dinner and a party at the splendid Grosvenor House Hotel in Park Lane. Neil told everyone he met, 'We won – I always said we would' – which is true, he did, and he had his picture taken with the award and got everyone to sign his menu.

At 3 a.m. he went to bed, and at 7.15 a.m. Lou Macari's mobile rang. It was BBC Radio Stoke. Would Lou please go along the corridor of his hotel and wake Neil, so that the radio station could interview him? No, said Lou understandably grumpily, and went back to sleep. A while later, Neil rose, ready to deal with the media, and ITN turned up to interview him while he was having breakfast.

On the way back to Stoke, Malcolm told him that, with the last game of the season coming up at Stoke, they might want him to go on the pitch and be cheered by the fans. 'I won't be there,' said Neil. 'I've promised to preach at Crick.' And he wasn't, despite the fact that Toby Jones was there as a guest of honour and was interviewed on the pitch. That's Neil. Yes, he loves glittering occasions, he loves celebrity and glamour, but he keeps them in proportion. If he has promised to do something, then it doesn't matter how glittering the subsequent invitation may be, he won't let people down.